PREACHING AND BIBLICAL THEOLOGY

Preaching
and
Biblical Theology

by
EDMUND P. CLOWNEY

Presbyterian and Reformed Publishing Co.

Nutley, N. J.

1975

PREFACE

BETWEEN THE STUDY AND THE PULPIT there seems to be a great gulf fixed. Preaching professors and scholarly preachers are exotic specimens in America, often betraying by their speech a British or Continental origin. Preachers-turned-professors labor under a double suspicion, but they do have at least a taste of two worlds. From such an experience this book has grown. A decade in the pastorate brought on me a dawning conviction that the biblical-theological approach of the seminary classroom was excitingly rich for the pulpit ministry. The renewed opportunities for study offered by seminary teaching have provided an excursion into an Aladdin's cave of treasures. (Or rather, in the imagery of biblical theology, a treasure city of Solomon, suggesting the inexhaustible riches of God's grace, hid in Christ!) The half cannot be told, but in this day of good tidings the wealth of biblical theology ought not to be buried on the study desk.

Chapter One seeks to define biblical theology. It has a much more specific meaning than the association of two such familiar words would suggest.

Chapter Two raises the question of the authority of preaching. What is meant by calling preaching *kerygmatic?* What theology of the Word underlies preaching? Questions of ultimate importance for the pulpit ministry are at the core of contemporary discussion in biblical theology.

The perspective of preaching is discussed in Chapter Three. Our proclamation is at the end of the age and to the ends of the world. It requires joyful boldness as well as desperate urgency. The richness of the message is its focus on Jesus Christ. Biblical theology presents the Christ of the Scriptures, and the depth of religious experience which responds in faith to him. 55230

Chapter Four relates biblical theology to the immediate

5

content of sermons, and ventures suggestions on tools and methods.

The substance of this book was delivered as three lectures in Grand Rapids, Michigan, June, 1956, to the Ministerial Institute of the Christian Reformed Church, a communion which has never divorced the pulpit from the study.

Particular thanks are due to my colleagues and students at Westminster Theological Seminary, whose interest and discernment in biblical theology are very imperfectly reflected in this book. I should like to thank particularly Miss Dorothy Newkirk for her skill and intelligence in typing the manuscript. All biblical quotations are taken from the American Standard Version except for a few instances where I am responsible for the translation.

EDMUND P. CLOWNEY

Westminster Theological Seminary
Philadelphia, Pennsylvania

CONTENTS

CHAPTER ONE

WHAT IS BIBLICAL THEOLOGY?

EVERY PREACHER who does not get his sermons from a book wants to put them into one. This guarantees an unfailing stream of sermonic literature, but it hardly accounts for the flood level of current books on preaching. The unspectacular work of the pulpit is exciting remarkable interest in a perverse age of jitters and yawns, when people may look, but seldom listen.

The behavioral scientists appear to be attending the church of their choice these days, and their analyses have further stimulated a reviving discussion among the preachers themselves. A minister must master pastoral psychology for "life-situation" preaching; if he cannot afford psychoanalysis, he must at least adopt counseling techniques to achieve empathy in the pulpit. Sociologists, too, have discovered the minister, and are systematically charting his conflicts as he insists on remaining a preacher in the midst of a dozen other roles thrust on him. Group studies of the congregation by these scientists may further inform and dismay the man in the pulpit, and the new field of communications spreads its network at his feet. From the ecumenical movement he learns of the ecclesiastical setting of preaching; bewildered though he may be by the latest book on symbolism, he is convinced that preaching must be related to worship and the sacraments.

Underlying these new concerns are the old and fundamental issues that have been forgotten rather than resolved. To relate preaching to our time we must know what preaching is and what it declares. By far the most important questions for the contemporary ministry of the Word are theological. The growth of what has been called a new "consensus" in theology has been the direct or contributing cause of much of the current revival of interest in preaching. In particular, the renewed attention to biblical studies touches both the nature and content of preaching at its heart.

Nothing is so essential for the preacher as that he should grasp, and be grasped by, the truth. Gaining a deeper insight into the meaning and the structure of God's revealed Word equips the man of God anew for every good work. In all the wealth of fresh approaches to preaching there is none which has the significance or usefulness of that development in biblical studies which is generally called biblical theology.

What is meant by biblical theology? Despite the fact that it is a recognized division of the modern theological field, this question proves extraordinarily difficult to answer. One finds articles and monographs of considerable complexity devoted to just this problem.[1]

At times the expression is used as a simple synonym for *Christian* theology, which, in its classical development at least, has always sought to give systematic formulation to the teaching of the Bible. The history of the term, however, gives it a more specialized meaning. At first it described the study of the biblical passages that support the divisions of dogmatic theology. German Pietists turned this phrase to polemic advantage by using it as a name for their own dogmatics. They contrasted their "biblical theology" with the speculative scholasticism of Lutheran orthodoxy. The term was then taken up by the rationalists of the Enlightenment, who identified biblical theology with the historical study of biblical religion. As Abraham Kuyper has pointed out, these rationalists did not *believe* the biblical theology they developed; rather they set it over against the confessional theology of the church so that they might be free to reject

---

1. A valuable introduction to recent literature on this whole question may be found in a survey article by William R. Baird, Jr., "Current Trends in New Testament Study," *The Journal of Religion*, XXXIX (1959), 137-153.

For further survey material, in addition to the bibliography furnished by Baird, see page 122 of this study.

both and go on to formulate their own rational theology.[2]

Unfortunately the term "biblical theology" still bears the stamp of this usage. For example, Professor Dentan of Yale observes with respect to this period, "No biblical theology in the modern sense of the term was possible until scholarship generally had abandoned the old hermeneutic principles of *analogia scripturae* and *analogia fidei,* which assumed both the uniformity of religious ideas in the Scriptures and their identity with the doctrines of the orthodox churches."[3]

The rationalistic principles, however, as they were developed through the nineteenth century, particularly in conjunction with the Hegelian philosophy of history, led to what has been called the suicide of the discipline. Kaehler remarks, "In glancing over the development of Biblical theology, it is surprising to see how this branch has worked out its own disintegration."[4] The inherent relativism of the historical method dissolved the concepts "biblical" and "theological," for the normative element essential to each was denied. The logical conclusion of this, made evident in the "history of religions" approach, was that the documents of the Old and New Testaments could not be distinguished from the literature of the ethnic religions, nor the religion of Israel from that of the surrounding nations.

Since World War I and Karl Barth's *Commentary on the Epistle to the Romans,* there has been a reaction to this extreme.[5] We are frequently assured today that the normative element is essential for biblical theology. With this emphasis there has come a revival of interest in the study of biblical theology. But while many are agreed that the normative must be restored, the manner of its restoration has proved to be a problem. Most modern scholars are not willing to return to the analogy of Scripture, for they deny

2. Abraham Kuyper, *Encyclopaedie der Heilige Godgeleerdheid* (Kampen, 1909), III, 170.

3. Robert C. Dentan, *op. cit.,* p. 6.

4. Martin Kaehler, *op. cit.,* p. 184.

5. This trend has been described in many of the articles cited on pages 122-124. See for example those written by J. D. Smart.

that the Bible presents a self-consistent standard. Some seek normative unity in a persistent and deep religious experience on the part of ancient Israel, shared by the Christian church. Others would find it in the redemptive actions of God, which have a continuity more or less faithfully reflected in the memorial records. In this last sense G. Ernest Wright declares, "Biblical theology, therefore, must be defined as the confessional recital of the acts of God in a particular history, together with the inferences drawn therefrom."[6]

The continuance of lively debate as to the "possibility" of a biblical theology[7] reflects the inconclusiveness of these efforts to affirm the normative unity of biblical theology after denying the normative unity of the Bible. Scholars who think there are many different theologies in Scripture (or the raw materials for many)[8] have surrendered the *biblical* basis for the unity of biblical theology. They may continue to seek theological unity by distilling it from the religious experiences of Israel, or perceiving it with the insight of the "mind of faith," but the result is not biblical theology in the proper sense of the term. Even the appeal to the redeeming and revealing actions of God as the foundational unity for biblical theology does not succeed in securing an objective source of unity in the Bible if it denies the unity of the Bible itself. One may believe that the many divergent responses in an all-too-human record were stimulated by a consistent pattern of divine action, but that belief remains empty unless this divine pattern is somehow perceived in the content of the recorded response. Apart from such content we cannot even affirm that we share with the Hebrew prophets the conviction that God acts. It may be that our god is their Baal.

As these critical scholars do grapple with the contents of

6. G. Ernest Wright, *op. cit.*, p. 156; cf. H. Wheeler Robinson, *Record and Revelation* (Oxford: Clarendon Press, 1938), pp. 315f.

7. See especially the symposium by J. R. Branton *et al.* in *Religion in Life* cited on page 122.

8. Gerhard Ebeling, "The Meaning of Biblical Theology," *Journal of Theological Studies*, N.S., VI (1955), 210-225.

the Bible, their own presuppositions become evident. Often it is apparent that they have replaced the analogy of Scripture with an analogy of the modern consciousness. Sometimes they assume that special revelation is continuing, so that our contemporary experience of "revelation" can correct the prophets[9]; often they confuse inspiration and illumination, to the devaluation of Scripture and the inflation of modern insights.

Bultmann's open demand that the message of the Bible must be demythologized is a consistent expression of the presuppositions of this whole approach. If there are no revealed truths, but only an encounter in the existential act of revelation, then the modern mind and not the Bible must supply the normative standard in understanding this encounter.

If we are to have a genuine biblical theology, however, we must accept biblical presuppositions and reject the anti-supernaturalism that is so often assumed to be inherent in the historical method. It is futile to give free scope to the negative criticism of such a method and then hope to build a biblical theology either with the remaining rubble or in the clouds of a noumenal dimension where faith has fled from science.

Biblical theology is a contradiction in terms unless the Bible presents a consistent message. Its essential presuppositions are the principles of revelation and inspiration claimed and assumed in the Bible itself. This is clearly seen and stoutly asserted by Geerhardus Vos in the introduction to his *Biblical Theology*.[10] He lays down as his first principle "the recognition of the infallible character of revelation as essential to every legitimate theological use made of this term."[11] He rightly contends that this is of the essence of theism. "If God be personal and conscious, then the inference is inevitable that in every mode of self-disclosure He will make a faultless

---

9. This, in my judgment, is what R. M. Brown does in the symposium cited on page 122.

10. G. Vos, *Biblical Theology* (Grand Rapids: Eerdmans, 1948).

11. *Ibid.*, p. 20.

expression of His nature and purpose. He will communicate His thought to the world with the stamp of divinity on it. If this were otherwise, then the reason would have to be sought in His being in some way tied up in the limitations and relativities of the world, the medium of expression obstructing His intercourse with the world."[12]

It is now a common assumption that revelation cannot consist in the communication of revealed truths. This conviction is not itself derived from the Bible. According to the biblical record, God could and did communicate revealed truths through all the prophets and finally through his Son, who came with the words that the Father had given him (John 17:8).

Vos emphasizes that biblical theology must recognize the objectivity of revelation. "This means that real communications came from God to man *ab extra*. It is unfair to pass this off with a contemptuous reference to the 'dictation' view. There is nothing undignified in dictation, certainly not as between God and man. Besides, it is unscientific, for the statements of the recipients of revelation show that such a process not seldom took place."[13] Vos goes on to make clear that he does not deny revelation from within. This is prominently present in the Psalms. However, Vos warns against the tendency to reduce all revelation in Scripture to this category in such a way as to deprive Scripture of its infallibility. "A favorite form is to confine revelation proper to the bare act of self-disclosure performed by God, and then to derive the entire thought-content of the Bible from human reflection upon these acts. Such a theory, as a rule, is made a cover for involving the whole teaching of the Bible in the relativity of purely human reflection, whose divine provenience cannot any longer be verified, because there is nothing objective left to verify it by."[14]

Recognizing the objectivity of revelation, Vos defines

12. *Ibid.*
13. *Ibid.*
14. *Ibid.*, p. 21.

biblical theology as "that branch of exegetical theology which deals with the process of the self-revelation of God deposited in the Bible."[15] Thus conceived, biblical theology is not self-contradictory. It does not undermine theology in the name of history. On the other hand it is not a reluctant concession on the part of orthodoxy to the demands of historical science.

It might be objected that if liberalism makes biblical theology impossible, orthodoxy makes it unnecessary. If propositions are given by revelation and a Book is the inspired Word of God, what does the church need beyond dogmatic theology as a compendium of biblical teaching and a system of proof texts to support it?

The form of the inscripturated Word itself gives answer to this question. The Bible records revelation given in the course of history. This revelation was not given at one time, nor in the form of a theological dictionary. It was given progressively, for the process of revelation accompanies the process of redemption. Since redemption does not proceed uniformly but in epochs determined by God's acts, so revelation has an epochal structure, manifested and marked in the canonical Scriptures. Modern dispensationalism rightly recognizes that there are great divisions in the history of redemption; it errs in failing to grasp the organic relation of these successive eras, as developing manifestations of one gracious design.

Biblical theology formulates the character and content of the progress of revelation in these periods, observing the expanding horizons from age to age. So understood, biblical theology is both legitimate and necessary. It provides the full context for the exegesis of particular passages, which must be understood not only in the setting of a book, but also in the "horizon" of a period of revelation. In the reciprocity characteristic of sound hermeneutics, biblical theology is also the fruit of exegesis, an essential step in the formulation of

15. *Ibid.*, p. 13.

summary statements concerning the teaching of the Bible as a whole.

There is, then, no opposition between biblical theology and systematic or dogmatic theology, though the two are distinct. Systematic theology must draw from the results of biblical theology, and biblical theology must be aware of the broad perspectives of systematics. The two approaches differ in the development of material. The development of systematics is strictly thematic or topical. It seeks to summarize the total teaching of Scripture under certain "loci" — of God, man, salvation, the church, the "last things." The development of biblical theology is redemptive-historical. The divisions of biblical theology are the historical periods of redemption, marked by creation, the fall, the flood, the call of Abraham, the exodus, and the coming of Christ. Within these periods, or within further sub-divisions of them, a systematic method is used. This is not merely systematic theology on the installment plan, however. It would be arbitrary to classify the revelation of each period under the same fixed divisions which best serve systematic theology. Rather, there must be a sensitivity to the distinctiveness and emphasis of both the form and content of revelation in each particular epoch. The theophanic revelations of the patriarchal period and the memorial altars bearing commemorative divine names have their rationale in form and content. The framework of interpretation must reflect this. Quite another organization of material is needed in dealing with the institutions of the theocracy. Biblical theology must understand each in its own terms, and see the theological significance of the progress from Jacob's ladder to Moses' tabernacle.

No doubt there is room for flexibility of organization. A scholar may write an "Old Testament Theology" in which the organization is topical and systematic rather than historical, but which justifies its title by tracing the development of each of the doctrines through the history of revelation before Christ. Such a treatment would bring biblical theology close to the form of systematics. Yet it would be well to avoid the confusion of understanding biblical theology as either "a systematic statement of what the Bible contains,"[16] or as the history of religious thought among the Hebrews.[17] The most fruitful understanding of biblical theology is that which recognizes both the historical and progressive character of revelation and the unity of the divine counsel which it declares. Its interest is not exclusively theological, because then the history of the revelatory process would be comparatively incidental. Neither is its interest exclusively historical. Those who propose that it be a history of Hebrew religion manifest a basic misunderstanding of revelation, or a disbelief in it. It is not precisely even a history of revelation, for its theological concern carries it beyond any merely historical study of the course of revelation.[18]

Biblical theology as a distinct and fruitful study must take seriously both historical progression and theological unity in the Bible. The old "proof-text" approach has been much caricatured; its use by men who knew and loved the Scriptures never even approximated the calculated perversion practiced by some modern cults. The Westminster divines, for example, were too familiar with their Bibles and with the exegetical labors of John Calvin to ignore the context when they were required to furnish scriptural "proofs."

Yet it cannot be denied that this approach often lacked depth in its use of the Bible. The emphasis on history so

16. James Muilenburg, "Is There a Biblical Theology?" *Union Seminary Quarterly Review,* XII:4, p. 31.

17. William A. Irwin finds it difficult to discover substantial differences between Old Testament theology and the history of the religion of Israel. He concludes that the chief distinction of the theological approach, in addition to a topical arrangement, is that it portrays Hebrew religious thought rather than practice and is concerned chiefly with the "higher" and therefore later manifestations of Hebrew religion. "The Reviving Theology of the Old Testament," *Journal of Religion,* XXV (1945), pp. 244ff.

18. Abraham Kuyper prefers to speak of *historia revelationis* rather than biblical theology, but he would include in dogmatic theology the tracing of the development of each doctrine through the history of revelation. *Op. cit.,* p. 175.

characteristic of nineteenth-century thought has brought a fresh appreciation of history in understanding Scripture. The tragedy is that from the same sources has come an understanding of history that is completely unscriptural, sharing the presuppositions of positivistic science. The critical scholar is given every right to "his primary supposition . . . that every sentence of every page of every manuscript of every book of the Bible has had an understandable historical provenance."[19] Since direct supernatural revelation — the voice of the Lord speaking from Sinai — is usually regarded as anything but an "understandable historical provenance," it is clear at what price "the Bible has been brought into organic relationship with the modern scientific conception of history."[20]

A biblical theology which accepts historical progression in such terms has surrendered any hope of setting forth the theological unity of the Bible. There may be efforts to maintain such a unity by constructing a non-historical dimension for "the history of salvation" (*Heilsgeschichte*), but such dualism is no solution of the dilemma. Biblical theology as a discipline has been cultivated by liberals, but the field of Bible study to which it has led the way requires the orthodox conviction that the Bible is God's supernatural revelation and has the unity of his Word. Unless the Scriptures actually possess the unity which biblical theology must find to justify its existence, the whole enterprise is folly.[21]

On the assumptions that the Bible itself makes, however, biblical theology is both proper and rewarding. The preacher who takes up Vos's *Biblical Theology* for the first time enters a rich new world, a world which lifts up his heart because he

19. A. C. Craig, *Preaching in a Scientific Age* (New York: Scribner's, 1954), p. 34.

20. *Ibid.*

21. W. A. Irwin is effective in objecting, particularly against Eissfeldt, to any attempt to select from the Bible only the elements congenial to a certain theological commitment and calling the result "biblical theology." *Op. cit.*, pp. 239ff.

is a preacher. Biblical theology, truly conceived, is a labor of worship. Beside Vos's *Biblical Theology* should be set his little book of sermons, *Grace and Glory*.[22] There we hear a scholar preaching to theological students (the sermons were delivered in Princeton Seminary), but with a burning tenderness and awesome realism that springs from the grace and glory of God's revelation, the historical actualization of his eternal counsel of redemption.

An old Dutch preacher has sagely observed that the pulpit must not drive us to the text, but rather the text must drive us to the pulpit.[23] In biblical theology that scriptural dynamic impels the preacher's heart with unimagined strength.

22. G. Vos, *Grace and Glory* (Grand Rapids, 1922).
23. J. van Andel, *Vademecum Pastorale* (Kampen, 1910), p. 36.

CHAPTER TWO

BIBLICAL THEOLOGY AND THE AUTHORITY OF PREACHING

Kerygma is the fashionable word for the message of the Christian pulpit. Along with other Greek terms, it has been restored by biblical theology to the preacher's working vocabulary. Its use is not pedantic if it stamps a fresh mint mark on our worn homiletical terminology. This New Testament noun for preaching implies that the gospel is a royal proclamation and the preacher an official messenger; the *kerygma* is the message of the King's herald. It describes the work of the preacher in apostolic contrast to jovial flippancy, highflown speculation, sentimental gush, moralistic nagging, and a dozen other abuses of the pulpit. Nor can it be applied readily to such sermon substitutes as book reviews, interpretative dancing, panel discussions, feature movies, or baptized vaudeville.

"Kerygma" in Modern Theology

Indeed, *kerygma* brings us again to the challenge of authority. This issue, which has kept modern biblical theology defending its existence, has been unavoidable in the development of its content. Any serious examination of the Bible must reckon with its constant claim to authority. Study on the scale and competence of Kittel's massive *Theological Dictionary of the New Testament*[1] has naturally aroused a new degree of appreciation for this subject. The article on *kerygma* and its cognates in this work is a leading example of the interest

---

1. Gerhard Kittel, ed., *Theologisches Wörterbuch zum Neuen Testament* (Stuttgart: Kohlhammer, 1933-).

20

quickened by biblical theology in the authority of preaching.[2]

These biblical studies have influenced contemporary theology, but it is no less true that theological interest in preaching has spurred and patterned investigation of the *kerygma* in Scripture. H. H. Farmer has stated that the most central trends of contemporary theology may be defined as "the rediscovery of the significance of preaching."[3] Barth's "theology of the Word" was developed in connection with his anxiety about preaching, and is centered upon "church proclamation" in sermon and sacrament. The movement he represents has therefore been called "*kerygmatic* theology."[4] Many recent discussions of *kerygma* have been related to the position of Rudolf Bultmann, who combines New Testament scholarship with a strong interest in theological and philosophical questions. He seeks to emancipate the *kerygma* from the "mythology" of the New Testament so that it may confront modern man as proclamation.[5]

The development in New Testament studies leading to the present emphasis on *kerygma* reflects these theological trends and the struggle between positivistic science and Scripture which underlies them.

Before the world wars, the "quest for the historical Jesus" held the interest of many scholars because it promised to disengage from the Gospels a Jesus in the liberal image, a humanitarian teacher and reformer who would authorize the liberal ideal. Gospel criticism assumed that the early church had entombed the man Jesus in a theological sarcophagus of divine Messiahship which must be broken away. The

2. Gerhard Friedrich in *op. cit.*, III (1938), 682-717.

3. H. H. Farmer, *The Servant of the Word* (New York: Scribner's, 1942), p. 9.

4. For example, by Paul Tillich, *Systematic Theology* (Chicago: University of Chicago Press, 1951), I, 4.

5. Rudolf Bultmann, "New Testament and Mythology," in Hans Werner Bartsch, ed., *Kerygma and Myth*, trans., Reginald H. Fuller (London: S.P.C.K., 1953), pp. 1-44. Cf. Philip E. Hughes, *Scripture and Myth* (London: The Tyndale Press, 1956).

attempt was unsuccessful. The tools of source criticism could uncover no other Jesus.[6]

Somewhat reluctantly the investigation turned from Jesus to the church. If the postulated "historical Jesus" could not be recovered, the New Testament was at least a primary source for information about the early "historical church." At first this development shifted attention from the Gospels to the Epistles and from Jesus to Paul. Later it yielded a new approach to the Gospels from a study of the early church. The method of "form criticism," which appeared after World War I, emphasized the formative role played by the oral tradition of the church in shaping the Gospels. Source criticism had sought literary documents behind the Gospels; form criticism concentrated on patterns of oral materials as alternative or prior sources. Passages (pericopes) were examined as to form on the assumption that habitual use in the preaching or teaching of the church had provided the setting in which they were shaped.

This approach, of which Bultmann was a leading exponent, was not without influence on C. H. Dodd as he developed his analysis of the *kerygma*.[7] Studying Paul's summaries of his preaching in his epistles and the sermons reported in Acts, Dodd identified certain common elements in the apostolic

6. Albert Schweitzer's *The Quest of the Historical Jesus* (trans. W. Montgomery, second Eng. ed., London, A & C. Black, 1926) showed that the apocalyptic views so repellent to the older liberalism could not be separated from the "Jesus of history." The issue is succinctly put by C. H. Dodd, *The Apostolic Preaching and Its Developments* (London: Hodder & Stoughton, 1936), pp. 182f. For surveys of these developments, see the literature cited on pages 122-124, especially J. M. Robinson, *A New Quest of the Historical Jesus;* A. M. Hunter, *Interpreting the New Testament;* and the article by W. R. Baird, Jr. See also Henry J. Cadbury, "Current Issues in New Testament Studies," *Harvard Divinity School Bulletin,* XIX (1953-1954), 49-64; William D. Davies, "A Quest To Be Resumed in New Testament Studies," *Union Seminary Quarterly Review,* XV (1960), 83-98.

7. Dodd, *loc. cit.* Dodd is critical as well as appreciative of Bultmann. For a brief resume by Dodd, see "Thirty Years of New Testament Study," *Religion in Life,* XIX (1949-1950), 323-333.

kerygma, all centered upon the arrival of the messianic age as the *eschaton,* the time of fulfillment promised by the prophets. This "realized eschatology" Dodd found to be essential to the apostolic preaching.

Dodd's view further contrasts "realized eschatology" with the futurist eschatology of apocalypticism. He argues that the church faced a critical situation in its first few years when the eschatological age did not immediately issue in the consummation. Two responses were possible: to stress the apocalyptic expectation of the second coming, or to discover a spiritual realization of all the promises in the present power of the kingdom. Dodd finds both responses in the New Testament, but emphasizes the latter. He sees in John's Gospel a spiritual interpretation of the kingdom as realized eschatology. The didactic material in Matthew he regards as another effort of the church to adjust to a situation in which the *eschaton* did not assume the form anticipated in the earliest *kerygma.* With the apocalyptic solution Dodd has little sympathy. The second coming is at best "the least inadequate myth," expressing by the fiction of an absolute end to history "the reality of teleology within history."[8]

Dodd's analysis of the *kerygma* has been profoundly influential, particularly in the English-speaking world. His distinction between the fundamental proclamation (*kerygma*) and the later teaching based upon it (*didache*) is most congenial to the activism of modern theology. The dynamic proclamation of redemptive event is to be contrasted with static systems of doctrine. For Dodd, the *kerygma* is associated with the divine initiative in judgment and grace, while the *didache* expresses the human response.[9]

Such a division puts a weight of authority on the *kerygma* which the *didache* cannot share. The *kerygma* itself, however, is not regarded as an objective deposit of authoritative reve-

8. Dodd, *The Apostolic Preaching,* pp. 240, 201.

9. "The Relevance of the Bible," in Alan Richardson and W. Schweitzer, eds., *Biblical Authority for Today* (Philadelphia: Westminster Press, 1951), p. 158; cf. *The Apostolic Preaching,* p. 6.

lation. It is not as though the Scriptures were to be divested of didactic accretions so that a remaining kerygmatic core might possess the full authority of *scriptura sola*. Rather, the *kerygma* is dynamically understood. Kerygmatic proclamation is an event in which God addresses his people. The authority is not in the *kerygma* as such, but exists through the divine action in the kerygmatic event.

The scholarly attempt to reconstruct the pattern of the earliest preaching does not therefore proceed on the assumption that this *kerygma* is the authoritative norm for our gospel. The historical Jesus believed much that modern man does not wish to accept. Modern theology is therefore zealous for the "Christ-event" as the norm rather than any actual words or deeds of Jesus of Nazareth. Similarly, the earliest *kerygma* was saturated with the apocalyptic supernaturalism that it derived from the teaching and work of Jesus. The primitive *kerygma* is no more acceptable to this modern mind than the historical Jesus.

No one puts this issue more plainly than Rudolf Bultmann. He insists that no modern man can seriously hold to a mythical world view which allows for supernatural intervention in history. The New Testament presupposes this mythical view when it presents the event of redemption which is the subject of its preaching. The *kerygma*, therefore, as it may be found in the New Testament, is now incredible. The miracles of healing, the physical resurrection, the ascension, the second coming in the clouds, not to speak of the deity and pre-existence of Christ: these are all impossible for users of electric light and radio.[10]

Does this *kerygma* then have any meaning for modern man? Bultmann believes that it has, for he regards myth as a form of symbolical language which may be interpreted, and concludes that the New Testament invites "demythologizing."

Not all achieve Bultmann's "absolute clarity and ruthless

10. Dodd, *The Apostolic Preaching*, pp. 1-8.

honesty" in perceiving both the unified pervasiveness of New Testament supernaturalism and its flat contradiction of the modern assumption that the natural world and human nature are "immune from the interference of supernatural powers."[11] His solution, in principle, however, differs little from what might be called a modern consensus. His "demythologizing" is but a drastic application of the common assumption that the apostolic witness in preaching and Scripture must be fallible because it is human. The *kerygma* itself, therefore, must be distinguished from the form in which it is expressed. Bultmann, Dodd, and others emphasize "realized eschatology" in the New Testament as an indication that within the Scriptures itself the process of demythologizing has begun. This position too is now widely accepted. For example, the coming of Christ in the Spirit promised in John 14:18 is understood as the Second Coming demythologized. When Bultmann has stripped the *kerygma* of its mythology, he finds its core in the Christ-event, which occurs anew in proclamation. The kerygmatic becomes synonymous with the existential.[12]

The basic issue as to the authority of the *kerygma* is not to be found in the discussions as to the precise content of the apostolic preaching, nor in the debates as to the limits of demythologizing. It lies rather in the view of revelation that these discussions assume. Revelation itself has been demythologized in deference to what is understood as modern science. The miracle of a revealed word is rejected as impossible. Sentences cannot be given by revelation. William Temple summarized this position: *"From all this it follows that there is no such thing as revealed truth. There are truths of revelation, that is to say, propositions which express the*

11. *Ibid.,* p. 7.

12. Therefore according to James M. Robinson, *op. cit.,* the approach of modern existential historiography offers a second avenue to Jesus complementing that of the *kerygma*. Without accepting Jesus' concepts or those of his disciples who preached the apostolic *kerygma*, we may be challenged in our existence by the evidence of his intention, as that is sought by modern historical study. Cf. pp. 85ff.

*results of correct thinking concerning revelation; but they
are not themselves directly revealed.*"[13]

Revelation is identified with redemption and is seen as
an event of personal encounter. The verbal results of such an
experience are not so much products of revelation as by-
products; they may serve as witnesses to revelation, but they
are neither revelation nor directly revelatory. Frequently
appeal is made to the fact that *dabar* in Hebrew may mean
either "word" or "event." The inference appears to be that the
two concepts were indistinguishable to the Hebrew mind
and that we are justified in regarding all word revelation as
action revelation.[14] The concept of revelation is analyzed to
yield the same result. By a curious pattern of reasoning it
is inferred that because personal communion is more than

13. William Temple, *Nature, Man and God* (London: Macmillan,
1935), p. 317. Italics in original.

14. E.g., John Baillie, *The Idea of Revelation in Recent Thought*
(New York: Columbia University Press, 1956), p. 81, where reference
is made to J. D. A. Macnicol, "Word and Deed in the Old Testament,"
Scottish Journal of Theology, V (1952), 247. See also Donald G. Miller,
Fire in Thy Mouth (New York: Abingdon, 1954), p. 24, where reference
is made to Hjalmar Lindroth, *En Bok am Bibeln* (Lund, 1948), p.
191, in *Source Material Study*, No. 50G/112, World Council of Churches.
The emphasis on the spoken word is unambiguously clear in *dabar*,
as, for example, in the phrase "The Word of the Lord came unto . . . .
saying" (e.g., Jonah 1:1); consider the frequent linking of *dabar* with
'amar. For the relation of the meaning *matter, affair* to the more
primary meanings of *dabar* see the Brown, Driver, Briggs edition of
Gesenius' lexicon (Boston and N. Y.: Houghton Mifflin, 1907), pp. 182f.
Dabar means *matter* or *affair* in the sense of the thing about which one
speaks. It is not true that Hebrew thought subordinates words to
events. The reverse is more nearly true, particularly in the case of
the word of the Lord, for his Word determines all events, and no
Word of God is void of power. Cf. Gen. 18:14; Jer. 32:17, 27 in Hebrew
and Septuagint with Luke 1:37. The use of *rhemata* in Luke and Acts
furnishes interesting examples of the colorlessness of translating "things"
where "sayings" is required by the contextual reference to the spoken
word. See Luke 1:65; 2:17-19, 50, 51; Acts 5:32, 13:42.

mere communication, it is exclusive of communication.[15] The slogan "revelation is not communication but communion" expresses a false disjunction. Personal communion without communication is impossible between human subjects, and it is a strange conception of revelation in Christ which denies to him revelatory communication in making known the Father. The insistence on the revelation in Christ as sheer Event is really only a denial of the revelation in word which Jesus himself professed to give.[16] The consequences of this dynamistic concept of the *kerygma* as revelation-in-act are far-reaching. Authority is stripped from the words of Scripture and almost inevitably decisive authority is assigned to the church. Dodd contends for an "indissoluble unity of Bible and Church" as the seat of authority.[17] He indeed declares that the tradition of the church must not impose an arbitrary meaning upon the words of the apostles and prophets. "They are our 'fellow-citizens' in the people of God, and we allow them the *parresia* which belongs to the free citizen, and listen with a decent humility while they speak for themselves."[18]

The shift in the locus of authority could hardly be more

15. John Baillie, *op. cit.*, pp. 32f. declares: "The present wide acceptance in this country of the view that revelation is not merely *from* Subject to subject, but also *of* Subject to subject, and that what God reveals to us is Himself and not merely a body of propositions about Himself, owes much to the teaching of Archbishop William Temple . . . ." He then quotes Temple, "There is no such thing as revealed truth." The "not merely" is a strange preparation for "no such thing"! This is not an incidental slip of rhetoric. Earlier Baillie argues similarly: "If it is information at all, it is information concerning the nature and mind and purpose of God — that and nothing else. Yet in the last resort it is not information about God that is revealed, but very God Himself incarnate in Jesus Christ our Lord" (p. 28). This "last resort" is a distant and desperate one, for it asserts that in revealing himself to us God does not or cannot convey information. The further declaration that this is the biblical view of revelation would be astounding if it were not so familiar.

16. E.g., John 12:49; 17:8.

17. Richardson and Schweitzer, *op. cit.*, p. 160.

18. *Ibid.*

dramatically indicated than in this defense of the right of the apostles to speak their own piece in the "town meeting" of the church! The activistic concept of revelation cannot but challenge the founding of the church upon the apostles and prophets as the recipients of final revelation. The emphasis is shifted to the church understood as a continuing fellowship in which redemptive action repeatedly occurs. Unique though the witness of the apostles and prophets may be, its power and authority exist only in the event of church proclamation when the Word of God is revealed. Apart from this, the apostolic witness is but the static residue of a once living event.[19]

19. Barth does assign a distinctive place to the witness of the prophets and apostles. Their witness is appointed in revelation itself, and unlike the subsequent proclamation of the church, attests revelation "in its uniqueness and temporal limitation." The original "sign" of revelation, the humanity of Christ, was terminated by the ascension, but the "sign" of the witness of the prophets and apostles entered this gap (Church Dogmatics, I2, The Doctrine of the Word of God, trans. G. W. Bromiley, T. F. Torrance, Edinburgh: T. & T. Clark, 1956, p. 500). They heard revelation as we can hear it only through their voices (p. 506). Their function is the more indispensable since no revealed content may ever be separated from the form of their witness (pp. 492, 495).

There is a vast alteration of the character of apostolic and ministerial authority when the objectivity of revealed truth is given up, as Barth has done. An intolerable dominion of men is introduced, for we are all subjected, not to the written Word of God, but to the fallible, erroneous, sinfully human words of men. Barth insists that here alone, in this witness, we must listen for the Word of God, as the church has directed us (cf. p. 479). The apostolic witness so conceived is a poor substitute for the "sign" of Christ's humanity, unless that also is made sinfully human. The bondage of conscience involved in the absolute subjection to such witness is compounded by the similar function given to the witness of church proclamation. The balancing emphasis in Barth's position offers no relief from this difficulty. He urges that only in the event, as the Word of God is revealed through Scripture, is the authority present. The individual "can and should himself be obedient only to Holy Scripture as it reveals itself to him . . ." (p. 479). Yet the limitation to an imperfect and sinful witness remains, not only as to the identity of the witness which may become the Word of God, but in the human nature of any witness which does become the Word of God.

The current activism appears to give new significance to authority in preaching. Preaching is seen as the redemptive event in which the Word of God is present and the church is called into existence. Because it empties the written Word of normative authority, however, this view radically alters the authority of preaching as well. On the one hand, the authority is shifted from content to form. *No* spoken words may be identified with the Word of God; they may only become such in the revelatory act. On the other hand, this formal authority is freed from the restriction of any objective norm. Virtually *any* words spoken in the situation may become God's Word. The preacher is no longer bound to the Word of God written.[20]

This "dynamic" view of preaching has already encouraged sacramentalism. The "event" can surely occur in sacramental action as readily as in preaching. Indeed, if revelation is not communication, the verbal process of preaching constitutes a barrier not found in the liturgical action of the sacrament. The last stage of this line of thought is reached when it is suggested that preaching is effective only because it is sacramental, employing verbal symbols rather than water, wine, and bread.[21] The relation of Word and sacrament in

20. As against the older liberalism there is a marked trend among theologians to call for a return to preaching the Bible. Tillich emphasizes the place of the Bible, but makes it the source rather than the norm of theology (*op. cit.*, pp. 50f. and 158f.). Barth eloquently pleads for biblical preaching, and seeks to show that preaching must be bound to the Scriptures. However, for him the Scriptures are not the Word written, they contain no system of doctrine or consistency of progressive revelation. Rather they are fragmentary, inconsistent, and contradictory. Yet any of these conflicting Scriptures may become, in proclamation, the Word of God (cf. *op. cit.*, pp. 483f., 507-510).

21. This tendency, at least, appears in the writings of G. van der Leeuw. Cf. *Ways of Worship*, edited by Pehr Edwall, *et al.* (London: S.C.M. Press, 1951), pp. 224-230, and van der Leeuw's *Liturgiek* (Nijkerk: Callenbach, 1946). See also E. Shillito, "The Preaching of the Word" in Nathaniel Micklem, ed., *Christian Worship* (Oxford: Clarendon Press, 1936), p. 216: "In preaching, then, we are administering a

the theology of the Reformation is then precisely reversed. Once the sacrament was called the *verbum visible;* now preaching becomes the *sacramentum verbale.*

The Biblical Doctrine of the Word of God

Current discussions of the scriptural *kerygma,* in spite of their learning and value, have commonly failed to appreciate the implications of the biblical doctrine of the word of God. The authority of the written Word, which is unfolded in biblical theology as the basis of all authority in preaching, is denied or minimized. For a genuine renewal of authority in preaching, the biblical theology of verbal revelation must be studied.

There can be no doubt that the whole structure of New Testament preaching rested upon the conviction that the gospel fulfilled the authoritative Scriptures of the Old Testament. Dodd's work on the relation of the *kerygma* to the Old Testament bears the illuminating title: *According to the Scriptures: the Sub-structure of New Testament Theology.*[22]

In the climax of Luke's Gospel the risen Christ opens the Scriptures to his disciples and opens their minds to understand the Scriptures (Luke 24:32, 45). The two disciples on the road to Emmaus were sad and confused even after hearing of angels in the empty tomb because they were slow of heart to believe all that the prophets had spoken (v. 25). Before their eyes were opened to know the Lord, their minds were opened to understand his Word, and their hearts burned with the recognition that Moses and all the prophets had spoken of Christ in his sufferings and glory.

The first preaching of the resurrection is Christ's own exposition of the Old Testament. This, indeed, is not a new message on the lips of Jesus. "These are my words which

---

Sacrament. The preacher has not the same preparation to make as the priest. But it is not a less serious task to handle words in the name of God than to offer to men the Bread and Wine."

22. London: Nisbet, 1952.

I spake unto you, while I was yet with you, that all things must needs be fulfilled, which are written in the law of Moses, and the prophets, and the psalms, concerning me" (v. 44). Yet the message is renewed and realized in the fact of the resurrection. The witness of the disciples, on receiving the Holy Spirit, is to these things; not merely to the fact of the resurrection, which apart from the witness of Scripture would be regarded just as the other disciples regarded the report of the women, as an empty tale, but to the Word of God fulfilled in the resurrection glory of Christ.

This core of Christian preaching given by Christ himself to his disciples is expanded in the book of Acts, with the greatest fidelity to the pattern of interpreting Scripture. The structure and even the vocabulary of this passage moulds Luke's reports of the apostolic witness in Acts. Peter on Pentecost preaches the sufferings and glory of Christ from Joel and the Psalms. In the temple, after the healing of the lame man, Peter's proclamation is of Christ's sufferings: "But the things which God foreshowed by the mouth of all the prophets, that his Christ should suffer, he thus fulfilled" (Acts 3:18). Then Peter preaches the glory to follow: "Jesus: whom the heaven must receive until the times of restoration of all things, whereof God spake by the mouth of his holy prophets that have been from of old" (v. 21). Peter continues by quoting from Moses as to the messianic prophet and asserts: "Yea and all the prophets from Samuel and them that followed after, as many as have spoken, they also told of these days" (v. 24).

Paul's preaching in the synagogue at Thessalonica is summarized by Luke according to the same pattern: "Paul . . . for three sabbath days reasoned with them from the scriptures, opening and alleging that it behooved the Christ to suffer, and to rise again from the dead; and that this Jesus, whom, *said he*, I proclaim unto you, is the Christ" (Acts 17:2, 3). This was the whole burden of Paul's preaching; before King Agrippa he describes his message as "saying nothing but what the prophets and Moses did say should come; how that the

Christ must suffer, *and* how that he first by the resurrection of the dead should proclaim light both to the people and to the Gentiles" (Acts 26:22b, 23). Luke's report is confirmed by Paul's well-known summary of the gospel he preached: ". . . that Christ died for our sins according to the scriptures; and that he was buried; and that he hath been raised on the third day according to the scriptures . . ." (I Cor. 15:3, 4). So also Peter speaks of the Spirit of Christ in the prophets testifying "beforehand the sufferings of Christ, and the glories that should follow them" (I Pet. 1:11).

This preaching of the fulfillment of the Word of God carries evidential force. Paul seeks to persuade his synagogue hearers from the Scriptures that Jesus is the Christ. The appeals of the Gospels of Matthew and John to the Old Testament similarly adduce specific Scriptures which Jesus pointedly fulfilled.

Yet this pattern of word-fulfillment has deeper roots than apologetic interest, and even that is never a superficial "proof-from-prophecy." The Gospels attest that Jesus found in the Scriptures the law of his life. He came not to destroy, but to fulfill (Matt. 5:17). The Scriptures cannot be broken (John 10:35). They testify of him (John 5:39). The Son of Man must go as it is written of him (Matt. 24:24, 56).

From a rationalistic standpoint, the apologetic value of Jesus' fulfillment of prophecy is diminished to the extent that Jesus sought to accomplish this consciously and deliberately. This attitude would see nothing remarkable in the fact that Jesus' cry from Golgotha is in the words of a Psalm familiar to him. To the writers of the Gospels, however, and to Jesus himself, Jesus' deliberate fulfillment of all Scripture is of the essence of his messianic vocation. To be sure, the outward events are also ordered by the Word of God. The agony of accursedness in which Jesus cries, "My God, my God, why hast thou forsaken me?" is fearfully real; it is the reality of which the Psalmist's cry was a prophetic and typical foretaste (Matt. 27:46; Ps. 22:1). The thirst of the cross was also real, and not self-inflicted. Yet the cry of abandonment and of thirst are uttered that the Scripture might be fulfilled (John 19:28).

To the Gospel writers and to Jesus there was nothing artificial in the fact that the most intimate crises of the Messiah's spiritual experience found expression in the fulfillment of the precise letter of Scripture. If all the Scriptures testify of Christ, Christ also is subject to the Scriptures.

The double relation here involved is the necessary consequence of the dual work Christ came to perform. As Immanuel, God-with-us, Christ is the Lord. The Spirit who spoke in the prophets is his Spirit. He is the Alpha and Omega of his own counsel, the Yea and Amen to his own promises. But he who is the Lord of the covenant is also the Servant of the covenant. As the Servant he comes to do the will of him that sent him, and to fulfill his work and word. The divine and human natures of Christ are united in his person, manifested in his work and revealed in his word.

The roots of this Word-fulfillment pattern of New Testament preaching are deep in the Old Testament. There the concept of the word of God is a dominant motif. "That God reveals himself by his word is a truth confirmed by every one of the Old Testament books."[23]

God's Sovereign Word

The grandeur of God's sovereignty in his word is the background of the fulfillment of God's word in Christ. God's rule through his mere word of decree is a supreme manifestation of his deity.[24] "And God said, Let there be light:

23. Edmond Jacob, *Theology of the Old Testament*, trans. A. W. Heathcote and P. J. Allcock (London: Hodder & Stoughton, 1958), p. 127.

24. The concept of the power of the word as an attestation of deity was understood in the ancient Near East. This is apparent in the Akkadian epic of creation, where Marduk successfully destroys and creates a piece of cloth at his word, showing that his "decree is first among the gods." "Creation Epic" IV:1-30, *Ancient Near Eastern Texts Relating to the Old Testament*, ed. James B. Pritchard (Princeton: Princeton University Press, 1950), p. 66.

and there was light" (Gen. 1:3). The worlds which were framed by the word of God are sustained in the same way (Ps. 33:6-11). The storms and the stars obey his word (Ps. 107:25; 147:15-18; 148:8; Isa. 40:26).[25] Kingdoms rise and fall at his decree (Ps. 46:6; 2:5; cf. Isa. 11:4). The emphasis, however, is not so much on the sovereignty of God's word in nature or providence as on its authority in the history of redemption. The most dramatic instances of the power of the word in the world of nature and over the nature-religions occur in the course of God's deliverances of his people. The gods of Egypt are judged by God's word spoken through Moses as Israel is delivered; fire falls from heaven and rains descend at Carmel to recall Israel from the vanity of worshiping the storm-god Baal.

At every step in the history of redemption the sovereign power of God's word is manifested. Immediately after the sin in Eden the voice of God is heard in the wind[26] and God declares both the curse of righteous judgment and the blessing of grace. As the writer of Hebrews traces the history of faith (Heb. 11) he is also outlining the history of redemption by the word of God to which faith responds. Revelation attends redemption; indeed, redemption is by the revealed word of God. In the book of Genesis a pattern of three steps emerges: first, a prior revelation of promise and call; then redemption in fulfillment of the promise; and, finally, confirmatory revelation and teaching sealing the redemption. This is the case with Noah, Abraham, and Jacob, so that the pattern is well established before it appears as the structure of the great redemption from Egypt.

One most significant statement of the redemptive power of God's word is in the divine utterance to Abraham in connection with the promise of the birth of Isaac: "Is there

---

25. P. van Imschoot, *Theologie de L' Ancien Testament*, Tome I, *Dieu* (Paris; N. Y.: Desclée, 1954), p. 203.

26. For the translation "sea wind" rather than "cool of the day" in Gen. 3:8, see A. Van Deussen, "Historische werkelijkheid," in *Gereformeerd Weekblad* (Kampen, Netherlands), February 12, 1954.

a word too wonderful for Jehovah?" (Gen. 18:14). The promise that the barren and aged Sarah should have a son had occasioned the laughter of both Abraham and his wife (Gen. 17:17; 18:12), but the word of God in its determined season will accomplish the wonder and give a new laughter, "Isaac," to Abraham and Sarah. The whole of redemption is fore-shadowed in this declaration of the redemptive potency of God's word; the word of God to Abraham is repeated by the angel Gabriel to Mary when her faith staggers at a greater promise: "For no word from God shall be void of power" (Luke 1:37).

The redemption from Egypt is preceded by the word of promise given in the call of Moses at the burning bush (Exod. 3:4). This word rests in turn upon the earlier promise to the fathers (Exod. 3:6).

In the address of the divine word to the people, the media-tion of the prophet is appointed. Moses' demurral at the bush becomes the occasion for the clear delineation of the prophetic office (Exod. 4:10-16). The prophet is the mouth-piece of God: God puts his words in the prophet's mouth and teaches (the verb from which *torah*, law, is derived) him what to say. "By a prophet the Lord brought Israel out of Egypt, and by a prophet was he preserved" (Hos. 12:13).

Through the word of God the redemption is accomplished, "that he may perform the word which the Lord sware unto thy fathers, Abraham, Isaac, and Jacob" (Deut. 9:5). "At the mouth of the Lord" (Exod. 17:1) the people cross the sea and journey in the wilderness to Sinai, where God speaks from heaven the words of his law. The people are given the word of God to direct their covenant service, and they are taught in the wilderness testings "that man shall not live by bread alone, but by every word that proceedeth out of the mouth of God" (Matt. 4:4; Deut. 8:3).

The redemptive word triumphs not only over the Egyptian pursuit, but over Israelite rebellion. It will secure at last the promised mercies. "God is not a man, that he should lie, Neither the son of man, that he should repent: Hath he said,

and will he not do it? Or hath he spoken, and will he not
make it good? Behold, I have received *commandment* to
bless: And he hath blessed, and I cannot reverse it" (Num.
23:19, 20).

The conquest of Canaan and the subsequent history of
Israel in the land is the history of the Lord performing that
which he had spoken.[27] The curses and the blessings of the
law find their fulfillment, and the prophets with growing in-
tensity anticipate the latter days, after the blessing and the
curse (Deut. 30:1), when the promises shall find their final
realization.

Through this whole period the emphasis on the word continues to develop. In the establishment of the kingdom, with
God's name dwelling at Jerusalem, the law is observed, the
prophetic office is established in the court, and the praises
of God are sung in the temple. The blessing of Solomon
witnesses to the fulfillment of the word: "There hath not
failed one word of all his good promise, which he promised
by Moses his servant . . ." (I Kings 8:56). To the word of
promise and warning is added a rich manifestation of the word
of praise and wisdom. On the other hand, the revolt of the
ten tribes (which itself fulfills God's word of judgment)
opens the way for new manifestations of the sovereignty of
the word. Elijah and Elisha as ministers of the word become
the chariots of Israel and the horsemen thereof (II Kings
2:12; 13:14). In the theophany at Horeb, Elijah is shown
that the sovereignty of God's word appears not only in the
word of judgment witholding the rain, and in the word of
power consuming the altar at Carmel, but in God's secret
control of all history to the accomplishment of his redemptive
purpose. God need not appear in the whirlwind, the earth-
quake, or the fire. His coming is in his whispered word,
spoken to his prophet, by which even a heathen king is
raised up and Baalism destroyed.

All the prophets testify to the absolute power of God's
word. The exile is in execution of God's counsel, and it opens

27. Cf. the passages cited by P. van Imschoot, *op. cit.,* p. 204.

a vast panorama of history in which the heathen nations are first instruments of wrath in God's hand to judge his people, and at last, after suffering judgment in turn, are made to partake in the salvation of the last days. Above the perspective of rising and falling empires the majesty of God's creative word is exalted.

In proclaiming the sure triumph of God's redeeming and restoring word the prophets refer to the power of God in creation and in the great deliverance from Egypt (e.g., Jer. 32:17-23). The declaration of the omnipotent promise of grace given to Abraham is repeated: no word is too wonderful for the God of all flesh (Jer. 32:17, 27). The accomplishment of blessing is not merely foreseen, it is purposed in God's decree. "I have purposed, I will also do it" (Isa. 46:11). "Thus saith Jehovah who brings it about, Jehovah who plans it to accomplish it; Jehovah is his name" (Jer. 33:2). "Surely, as I have thought, so shall it come to pass . . ." (Isa. 14:24). The coming of the glory of the Lord is certain "for the mouth of the Lord hath spoken it" (Isa. 40:5), and "the word of our God shall stand forever" (v. 8). As the fructifying rain descends, "so shall my word be that goeth forth out of my mouth: it shall not return unto me void, but it shall accomplish that which I please, and it shall prosper in the thing whereto I sent it" (Isa. 55:11). As the flowering, fruit-bearing almond rod of Aaron sealed the word of God appointing his ministry, so the Lord will watch over his word to perform it (Jer. 1:12).

The climax of the promised salvation will come with the Messiah, formed from the womb to be the Servant of the Lord, not only to raise up Jacob and restore the preserved of Israel, but to be a light to the Gentiles (Isa. 49:5-6). His mouth will be like a sharp sword (Isa. 49:2); he cries, "The Lord Jehovah hath given me the tongue of them that are taught, that I may know how to sustain with words him that is weary" (Isa. 50:4). The word of the Lord and the law that shall go forth for a light of the peoples will be given through the Servant of the Lord (cf. Isa. 50:10; 51:4). "And

I have put my words in thy mouth, and have covered thee in the shadow of my hand, that I may plant the heavens, and lay the foundations of the earth, and say unto Zion, Thou art my people" (Isa. 51:16). Here the redemptive and creative word of God is ministered through the great Servant of whom Moses was the type (cf. the language of Exod. 33:22; Deut. 18:18). The isles of the Gentiles shall wait for his law (Isa. 42:4); he is anointed to preach the gospel to the meek and proclaim the climactic Jubliee, the year of the Lord (Isa. 61:1-3; Luke 4:17-21; Matt. 5:1-12).

In creation and redemption the dynamic, formative power of God's word is asserted with abundant emphasis. The association of God's word and Spirit is particularly close. Often the word is objectified and virtually identified with breath or spirit, as that which is gone forth from the lips.[28] It is also one with the thoughts and purposes of the heart. Men speak within themselves, or commune with their spirits. So God's thoughts and purposes are revealed and executed by his word.

However, the dynamism and spirituality of the word is not, in the Old Testament, in tension with the objectivity of the word. The creative word may be remembered or recorded. The power of the word of God has the mystery of God's own glory, but the wonder lies not in a power that the word has of itself, but in that God pronounced it and will watch over it to perform it.

The Word of God and the Covenant

The objectivity of the word comes particularly to expression in the doctrine of the covenant. The whole doctrine of the word in the Old Testament is determined by the covenant scheme, so that even God's word addressed to nature is expressed in covenantal terms and in connection with

28. Cf. Th. C. Vriezen, "God's Revelation by His Spirit and His Word," in *An Outline of Old Testament Theology,* Eng. tr. (Oxford: Blackwell, 1958), pp. 249ff.

covenantal blessings. (Cf. Hos. 2:21-23; Jer. 33:20, 21, 25; Gen. 9:9-17.)[29]

The inscripturation of the word of God occurs at Sinai with the establishment of God's covenant with his people. While God's calling of the fathers had a covenant form, the redemption of the assembly of God's people, the congregation of Israel, calls for a formal covenant ratification with a precise and objective covenant instrument in writing.

Recent studies of the covenant form in Hittite suzerainty treaties provide startling evidence of the importance of the written document in royal covenants of the ancient Near East, and illumine the covenant structure of the Pentateuch.[30] The source material studied is from the period of the Hittite Empire, about 1450-1200 B.C. The form was not original with the Hittites; rather it was common at least to the cultures of Palestine, Syria, and Asia Minor. In both time and place, therefore, these treaties are from the cultural horizon which forms the background to God's covenant-making with Israel. The basic form of the Hittite covenant was unilateral. It was a covenant bound upon a vassal by a king with an oath. It is spoken of as the sovereign's covenant; the specific obligations are his "words." The usual elements found in the texts of this covenant form (as summarized by Mendenhall) included: (1) A preamble, beginning "Thus [saith] NN, the great king . . ." and giving the titles, attributes, and genealogy of the monarch who confers the covenant relation upon his vassal.

(2) An historical prologue, describing the king's previous relations with his vassal. This is not stereotyped, but gives

---

29. Cf. Harold Fisch, "The Analogy of Nature, a Note on the Structure of Old Testament Imagery," *Journal of Theological Studies*, N.S., VI, 161-173.

30. The basic study of the Hittite treaties is by V. Korosec, *Hethitische Staatsvertraege* (Leipzig, 1931). The material was presented and analyzed in two most important articles in the *Biblical Archaeologist* by George E. Mendenhall, "Ancient Oriental and Biblical Law," and "Covenant Forms in Israelite Tradition," XVII (1954), 26-46, 50-76.

historical data and purports to show the king's claim upon
the vassal's gratitude. It is expressed in "I-thou" address.

(3) Stipulations, requirements of the vassal, including the
prohibition of alliances with other kings and the honoring
of the king's authority as judge.

(4) A provision for the deposit of the written covenant
in the sanctuary, and for periodic public reading.[31]

(5) A list of gods as witnesses.

(6) Formulas of curses and blessings.

Mendenhall has called attention to the many striking similarities between these covenants and God's covenant described
in Exodus and Joshua. Clearly, it is this covenant form which
is used in Exodus 20. God, the Sovereign, binds Israel to
himself in covenant relation. His claim upon them is seen
in his redeeming act, and in covenant jealously he forbids their
subjection to any other lord.

In exact conformity with the covenant customs of the
time, the covenant is written and deposited in a specially made
ark in the sanctuary of the tabernacle. It is this written form
which is a testimony, a witness, to the precise nature of the
covenant bond as well as its reality (Exod. 32:15; 34:29).
This is God's covenant, the words of Jehovah. He spoke
them from heaven, and the people heard. He recorded them
on the tablets of stone and Moses brought them down from
the mount. "And the tables were the work of God, and the
writing was the writing of God, graven upon the tables"
(Exod. 32:16). Although the suzerainty covenant did not
have the parity structure of a modern contract, the written
document was not less important. "And the Lord said unto
Moses, Write thou these words: for in these terms (*'al-pi
hadebarim*) I have made a covenant with thee and with
Israel" (Exod. 34:27). The tablets of stone are the tablets of

---

31. Meredith G. Kline accounts for the "two tables" of the law
in terms of the custom of making duplicate copies of treaties, one
for the sovereign, one for the vassal. Since in this case of God's covenant
with his people there was but one sanctuary, both copies were placed
in the ark. "The Two Tables of the Covenant," *The Westminster
Theological Journal*, XXII (1960), 133-146.

the covenant, or simply, Jehovah's covenant (I Kings 8:21; II Chron. 5:10; 6:11; cf. I Kings 8:9).

These tablets of stone in the ark are the heart of the Pentateuch. The brief historical prologue of the covenant at Sinai is the key to understanding the whole preceding history of Exodus, and the books of generations in Genesis as well. The history of the Pentateuch is not political or cultural in aim, nor is it a chronicle of stirring events. It is covenantal history: the record of God's dealings with the fathers, his covenant with Abraham and its renewal at Sinai. The force of covenant history lies in its actuality, its "historicity." It has been noted that the Hittite covenants did not present stylized generalities in the historical prologue, but recorded specific instances of the sovereign's gracious dealings with the vassal.

As the history of the Pentateuch is covenant history, so the law is the requirement of the covenant: "And Jehovah said unto Moses, Come up to me into the mount, and be there: and I will give thee the tables of stone, and the law and the commandment, which I have written, that thou mayest teach them" (Exod. 24:12). The law is the teaching (*torah*, cf. *horah*) of the way of the Lord to his people.[32] It is written in the book of the covenant (Exod. 24:4, 7; *cf.* Josh. 24:26).

The blessings and curses of the covenant, also present on the tables of stone, are expanded in Deuteronomy 27-28.

The complete book of the covenant, written by Moses, is placed in the Ark of the Testimony (Deut. 31:24-26). God's Word is present in the midst of his people (Deut. 30:11-14). By its presence the covenant assembly is constituted. The covenant structure, then, requires precise and objective written statements: the text of the covenant proper, with its stipulations; the identification of the covenant Sovereign and the genealogies of those with whom the covenant is made; the history of God's gracious dealings in the past which are motivations to gratitude for those who receive his covenant;

---

32. See Gunnar Ostborn, *Tora in the Old Testament* (Lund: Hakan Ohlssons Boktryckeri, 1945), pp. 38-41.

the record or annals of covenant service which memorialize faithfulness or unfaithfulness to the covenant; the threat of curse and the promise of blessing.

Yet the formal, legal objectivity of God's word given to his people is never opposed to the dynamic, creative power of God's word of decree.[33] A beautiful example of the harmonious relation between the two is found in Psalm 147: 15-20 where the word and commandment of God is described as sent upon earth to bring winter and springtime, and the declaration follows, "He showeth his word unto Jacob, his statutes and his ordinances unto Israel."

The attempt to trace a process of fossilization in the Old Testament by which a dynamistic, prophetic concept of the word hardened into a static legalism cannot succeed, even with the critical dating of books and "sources."[34] The book of Deuteronomy is, on this scheme, assigned to the seventh century, and its blending of law and prophecy is seen as a relatively late development. Yet, actually, the concept of the covenant which is the core of Old Testament revelation finds

33. Indeed, a closer relation may exist between the book of God's decrees and the book of the covenant than is usually recognized. The book of God from which Moses is willing to have his name erased for Israel's sake (Exod. 32:32; cf. Dan. 12:1), may be understood as the heavenly pattern and original of the book of the covenant. As the book of the covenant contains the names and genealogies of those with whom God's covenant is established, so God records the names of his people in his book of judgment, which is the divine book of memorial to the covenant (cf. Exod. 17:14; Mal. 3:16; Luke 10:20; Heb. 12:23; Ps. 87:6). The fascinating article by Henning Graf Reventlow, "Das Amt des Mazkir," *Theologische Zeitschrift*, XV (1959), 161-175, suggests that the "Recorder" of David's court was a covenant official, "bringing to remembrance" the covenant law, as a kind of attorney general, and compares this theocratic function with the divine recording and remembering.

For the combination of the dynamic and the recorded word without any sense of opposition in the Akkadian mythology, cf. the "tablets of fate" in the *Creation Epic*, III:5; IV:121 (Pritchard, *op. cit.*, pp. 65, 67).

34. Edmond Jacob, *op. cit.*, pp. 127-133; Th. C. Vriezen, *op. cit.*, pp. 86-96.

its background in the historical period in which Moses lived, and this pattern requires the objectivity, even the inscription, of the covenant text.

The antithesis between free spirit and fixed letter does not exist in respect to God's word in the Old Testament. The very concept of God's word excludes it. Since the word that goes forth from the lips of God the King cannot be altered or fail, its enduring permanence and objectivity are secured. From the earliest time there is no evidence that the word of God was ever conceived in other than objective terms. There was the danger of depersonalizing the word by debasing it to a magic formula, a path which was followed in Egypt, but the intimate connection of the Lord and his word seems to have prevented this abuse in Israel. Worship became formalistic, to be sure, but the concept of God's revelation in his word remained.

The same covenant form which stresses the objectivity of the word provides a dynamic setting as well. The covenant is inseparable from promise. The covenant relation is a life relation: I will be your God, and ye shall be my people (Lev. 26:11, 12). The covenant Lord dwells in the midst of his people. The legal aspect of the covenant is not abstract code, insulating the people from contact with the living God by a screen of legalism. It is *torah*, direction in the ways of the Lord. It reveals what is well-pleasing to God, so that he may dwell with his people and they with him (Deut. 4:1-14).

The covenant relation is itself a relation of blessing, but it is directed toward greater blessing. From the call of Abraham the promise aspect of the covenant is stressed. Through the covenant relation will come the restoration of all things, so that all the families of the earth will be blessed in Abraham (Gen. 12:3; 18:17-19). The covenant redemption will secure the realization of the ultimate covenant promises. The covenant of Sinai again has in view all the nations of the earth, among whom Israel is made a holy nation and a kingdom of priests (Exod. 19:5, 6). The theophany at Sinai is not the final revelation of God to his people, but points forward to the possession of the land, and the establishment of God's name in his sanctuary in Zion.

The blessings of the covenant are eschatological in character. As has been noted, the book of Deuteronomy looks beyond the initial realization of the covenant blessing and outpouring of the curse to the final triumph of blessedness by God's grace. This is the master-plan of the whole subsequent covenant history. In the symbolism of the ceremonial calendar the sabbath of the sabbaths of years must issue in the year of jubilee, the acceptable year of the Lord in which the covenant promises are realized.

God's declaration of his purposes before their realization is made a token of his covenant faithfulness. The demonstrated power of his word manifests the reality of the covenant bond. "Shall I hide from Abraham that which I do?" (Gen. 18:17). The Exodus deliverance fulfills the promise made to the fathers (Exod. 3:4) and reveals the covenant faithfulness and grace which are associated with the "memorial," covenant name of Jehovah. In his call to Moses God foretells the deliverance before he accomplishes it, so that the covenantal gathering at Sinai is itself a fulfillment of the promise and a "sign"; the redeemed nation worships God "upon this mountain" (Exod. 3:12).

The whole theology of the covenant centers on the faithfulness of God's grace. He remembers his covenant, not only in visiting judgment upon a covenant-breaking people, but in triumphing over rebellion to establish the purposes of covenant election. The infamous names of rebellion in the wilderness — Marah, Sin, Massah, Meribah — become witnesses to God's grace and covenant faithfulness. God's word is the word of his oath which will be fulfilled. The sign of the prophet is also the sign of the covenant: God's word comes to pass. Even the climactic rebellion which brings the covenant curse of exile is not the finale of the history of redemption. The former things are come to pass, "and new things do I declare; before they spring forth I tell you of them" (Isa. 42:9). God will reveal the hidden counsels of his mercy (Jer. 33:3) and renew his covenant in messianic blessing.

Just here many modern scholars misconstrue the biblical concept of the word in relation to preaching and its authority. It is foolish to deduce from the use of *dabar* that the Hebrews could not distinguish between word and event.[35] The whole structure of promise in the covenant, and with it the orientation of covenant faith, rests precisely upon this distinction. Abraham believed God. He had received the word but not the event. When the event fulfills the word, the promise is confirmed and faith rejoices in realization. Abraham's faith was realized in the birth of Isaac, and that event became a "sign" of God's faithfulness which strengthened Abraham's faith to rejoice in the coming of the day of Christ, the final Seed of the promise.[36]

So also the test of a prophet is twofold: faithfulness to the covenant God (Deut. 13:1-5), and the fulfillment of the prophet's predictions as a sign of God's word of power (Deut. 18:21, 22).

The amazing chain of reasoning that argues from the scriptural premise that the word of God is efficacious and active to the contradictory conclusion that it is an act rather than a word has no support whatever in the Bible. The theory of preaching based upon it is equally contradictory.[37] On the

---

35. See above, note 14.

36. Gunnar Ostborn observes: "However, the historical representations of the Old Testament are especially marked by the notion that Yahweh speaks before he acts. What happens in history, is, then, a fulfillment of what Yahweh has earlier spoken (e.g. Exod. 3:16f., 14:30f.; I Kings 8:56; Ezra 6:14; Isa. 14:26f., 55:11f.; Jer. 1:12; Ezek. 17:24; Dan. 4:28ff.). Yahweh's words as active in history thus appear to constitute a peculiar feature of Yahwism." *Yahweh and Baal* (Lund: C. W. K. Gleerup, 1956), pp. 102f.

37. Donald G. Miller in "Biblical Theology and Preaching" (*Scottish Journal of Theology*, XI, 1958, 389-405) stresses the "unresolved and unresolvable contradiction" (p. 391) of preaching. "We have argued that the Word of God is not words but his act, his deed. But then we have said that the Bible is the record of men's words about God's

other hand, the biblical theology of the word is grounded in the Lord's own speaking in words: in the garden, from the bush, from above Sinai.

On the great "day of the assembly" the covenant God speaks from the cloud and fire on the mountain top to his redeemed people gathered in the plain below. This is revelation in act, to be sure, but it is also revelation in word. The dread voice declares the words of the covenant. This scene makes nonsense of the contention that what God gives us in revelation is not information but himself, and that his method is not communication but communion.[38]

The covenant form, then, stresses the objectivity of the written word; as the form of revelation, it emphasizes the objectivity of the written word of God. Moreover, it implies a variety of written materials. The covenant includes history, genealogy, formulas of blessing and cursing, as well

---

deed, and that the essential thing in the church's ministry ought to be words about God's deed" (ibid.). "Biblical theology . . . deepens the contradiction growing out of the fact that God's true word is his act, but that men must talk about his act in words, thus changing its character entirely" (p. 392). The solution is that preaching, too, must become God's act, a human impossibility.

The incongruity of a sinful man being made a preacher of God's Word must indeed fill the minister with humble awe, but this is not heightened by confusing word and act. If we argue that because God's Word is act, the Bible cannot be God's Word in a strict sense, but only "men's words about God's deed," then surely we cannot preach God's Word, however much we might desire God to act in our preaching. Professor Miller's appeal to parallels in the Psalms to equate word and act overlooks the force of this correlation, which is to assert the power of God's Word and the fulfillment of his promise. Note, for example, Psalm 105:19, 42, 43.

38. See note 15 above. It is the denial of communication and of the giving of information that is false. Revelation leads to communion and may be given in communion, but it is not reducible to communion. That which the finger writes upon the wall is revelation, and its significance may be declared to those who are under its judgment and altogether outside of any communion with God (Dan. 5). Balaam as well as Moses may utter the Word of God.

as apodictic and casuistic law. The variety and unity of the materials of the Pentateuch are so to be understood. The records of covenant "memorials" kept by ancient sovereigns included not only the texts of covenant renewals, but also the royal annals recording vassal tribute and noting instances of obedience or rebellion. These would furnish a further figure of the book of the covenant kept by the Divine King, whether in heaven or through his word given to his servants the prophets.

However, the dynamic of the covenant is not restricted by the treaty forms and royal records of the ancient world. The character of the covenant itself has profound implications for the form of revelation. God dwells with his people. The covenantal presence of God requires the response of service. Even the reception of the covenant is in a service of worship (cf. Exod. 3:12; 8:1), and all of life is covenant service to the Lord. As the patriarchs were servants of the Lord, so the nation Israel is called as God's son to serve him. Serving the Lord in contrast with other gods is the distinctive requirement of the covenant constitution in Deuteronomy (6:13; 10:12; 11:13). This service is religious in character. It springs from the fear of the Lord, and is the attitude and response appropriate to that fear; not slavish terror, but awe and love (Deut. 4:10; 6:13; 10:20). It demands the whole heart (Deut. 10:12; 11:13) and is to be rendered with joy and gladness (Deut. 28:47). The service of ethical uprightness is included. The cultus of worship is expressive of this religious relation, and is covenantal in character. Particularly it brings to expression the spirituality of God (Deut. 4:15-24; 12:30; cf. 26, 27).

The response of such covenant service flows from the presence of God with his people. Here is the foundation for an answering word to the covenant command and promise. The word of worship, evoked from the lips of the covenant servant through the presence of God's Spirit, introduces another aspect of the authoritative word in the Old Testament. As the word of God comes in objective, memorable form, so the response evoked may be an inspired word, whether it is the word of a patriarch naming an altar where God's presence has been manifest, or the song of Moses, or the psalms of David.[39]

The modern emphasis joining revelation with worship has reflected some sensitivity to this covenantal pattern. An opposite conclusion needs to be drawn, however, from that generally adduced. The situation in worship, so far from detracting from the emphasis on verbal revelation, rather strengthens it. The glory of the covenant lies in God's speaking to his people. The climax of redemption is in their response. The spiritual word of address by God evokes the spiritual word of response in which God's holy name is lifted up in praise. That utterance of worship may be formed by the Spirit of God. Prophets not only proclaim the word of God. They also pray and praise in the ecstasy of the Spirit (Exod. 15:1; Deut. 31:19, 30, 31; II Sam. 23:1, 2; cf. Num. 11:26-29). God who breathed into man the breath of life will receive from man's lips the Spirit-filled worship of praise. God's word from heaven is the foundation of the covenant and of the biblical doctrine of revelation. The Spirit-filled response of the servant of God is the fulfillment of the covenant and manifests the richness of the word of God which is both call and answer.

The Ministry of the Word in the Old Testament

The ministry of the word springing from God's manifold revelation is twofold: first, there is a prophetic, mediatorial ministry of conveying God's words to the people. Because the people could not bear to hear the voice of God in thunder from above Sinai, Moses was called to receive the revelation

39. Note the description of Moses' song in the words of Jehovah, Deuteronomy 31:19: "Now therefore write ye this song for you, and teach thou it the children of Israel: put it in their mouths, that this song may be a witness for me against the children of Israel." The song blesses the name of God and admonishes the people. It forms part of the covenant instruction while it is also a covenant response. See II Samuel 23:1, 2.

and bring it to them (Exod. 20:19; Deut. 5:27-33). Included in this task is the work of inscripturation. In writing the book of the covenant Moses continues the work begun by the finger of God upon the tablets of stone. The mediatorial function of Moses becomes the pattern for the prophetic office. The law of the prophet in Deuteronomy 18:15-22 makes explicit reference to the request of the people at Sinai which led to Moses' prophetic mediation. Because a sinful people cannot abide his voice or the consuming fire of his presence, God will raise up the prophets and ultimately the Prophet, ". . . and I will put my words in his mouth, and he shall speak unto them all that I shall command him" (Deut. 18:18).

The second aspect of the ministry of the word is the teaching of the revealed word. As has been indicated, the very term *torah* points to this. The covenantal content of God's revelation requires that this word which has been brought near by revelation and inscripturation should be taught to the people, and to their children (Exod. 4:14-16; 24:12; Deut. 5:31). God's instruction out of heaven is written so that it may be taught by Moses, the priests, the prophets, the judges and the king (cf. Lev. 10:11; Deut. 31:10; 33:10; 17:8-13, 18-20; Neh. 8; I Sam. 12:23; II Chron. 17:7-19; Jer. 18:18; Mal. 2:7).

"The things that are revealed belong unto us and to our children for ever, that we may do all the words of this law" (Deut. 29:29). The faithful teaching of the revealed word inscribes it upon the hearts of fathers and children, that it may be obeyed (Deut. 30:11-14; cf. 6:6-9).

The teaching of the revealed word is closely associated with the reception of further revelation. The priests who are to teach the law are also to inquire of the Lord through the use of the Urim and Thummim (Num. 27:21), and the prophet both receives the word and ministers the word already given. The prophetic denunciations are directed at those who break the law both as given in the wilderness and through prophets after Moses (Jer. 9:12, 13; 16:11; 26:2-

6; 32:20-23; 44:10; Hos. 8:1, 12; 4:1-6; Amos 2:4; Isa. 42:24; Zech. 7:9-12).[40]

Throughout the Old Testament, however, a deposit of revelation is recognized which must be taught to God's people. In addition to the coming of the word of the Lord, which at times was interrupted, usually in judgment, there is the presence of the word already given. The work of Aaron in speaking to the people the word given through Moses (cf. Exod. 4:14-16) is a continuing requirement in Israel, however neglected or abused. The recovery of the book of the law (II Kings 22:8) and the renewed teaching of the law (II Chron. 17:7-19) bring revival to the people of God. Not only the prophets, priests, and princes of the people were responsible for teaching the word of God. Every father in Israel had this responsibility. The development of wise men and scribes is against this background of the revealed Word.[41] The teaching of Ezra the priest (Neh. 8) is the crowning example of the faithful discharge of this aspect of the ministry of the word in the Old Testament. It became the model for synagogue preaching, and our Lord followed the pattern in Nazareth when he proclaimed the fulfillment of Isaiah's prophecy in himself (Luke 4:16-21). With the completion of revelation in the gospel of Christ, this function became the sole and indispensable ministry of the word among God's people. The calling of the prophet is completed in the apostolic age, but that of the pastor and teacher remains.

Christ the Word

The Old Testament pattern of objective revelation and authoritative teaching is fulfilled but not destroyed in the coming of Christ. No suppression or sublimation of verbal revelation is involved in the work of the Messiah. In Jesus Christ, the word is not an uninterpreted act or a bare event but a *person*: One who acts, to be sure, but who also speaks.

40. Cf. Ostborn, *Tora in the Old Testament*, pp. 141ff.
41. Cf. Jacob, *op. cit.*, p. 132.

Christ the *Logos* is the full and final revelation of God in both word and deed (Acts 1:1). He fulfills the promise of the prophet in Deuteronomy 18:18.[42]

The prophetic office of Christ is evident in all of the Gospels. It is powerfully presented, for example, in the account of the Transfiguration in the Synoptics. The voice from the cloud on the mount declares: "This is my beloved Son: hear him" (Luke 9:35, A.V.). The force of this command is profound in the context. Moses the founder, and Elijah the restorer of the prophetic office appear on the mount with the glorified Christ. In deed and word it is Jesus only who remains. Yet the work that he must accomplish and the revelation he must give do not destroy but confirm and fulfill the law and the prophets.

Another and slightly less direct allusion to the work of Moses is found in the prayer of Christ in John 17:8. Here Jesus speaks of giving to his disciples the words (*rhemata*) which the Father had given him. As Moses on Mount Sinai received the words of the law, so the Son, in the glory which he had with the Father before the world was, received the words which he delivers to his people.

The authority (*exousia*) of Christ must be understood therefore against the background of the Old Testament. This accounts for the fact that the initial *kerygma* of Jesus is identical with that of John. John comes as a prophet in the Old Testament pattern and declares that the days of fulfillment are at hand. Jesus takes up this same prophetic work and proclaims this same message. Yet Jesus is more than a prophet. He is the fulfillment of all prophecy. Therefore his preaching that the kingdom is at hand is widened to the tremendous declaration in the synagogue of Nazareth, "Today hath this scripture been fulfilled in your ears" (Luke 4:21).

---

42. An important passage for the New Testament writers. Cf. C. H. Dodd, *According to the Scriptures,* p. 57. Dodd cites not only Acts 3:22ff., but also Luke 9:35 and John 6:14.

Christ's authority transcends the authority of Moses as the authority of the Son transcends that of the servant. God spoke directly from the cloud on Mount Sinai, then gave the law in further detail to Moses. From the theophanic cloud on the Mount of Transfiguration God does not give ten commandments but one: "This is my beloved Son: hear him." With the presence of the Son, God's message need no longer be proclaimed from the cloud. Seated on the mount in Galilee, the Messiah gives his *torah* in the majestic word of absolute authority, "I say unto you . . . ."

He that sees the Son sees the Father, and he that hears the words of the Son hears the word of God. The character of the office of Christ as the Messianic prophet can only be understood in the realization of the nature of his person as God the Son. The message of the Son is not one which he receives on a mount, as did Moses. His message is that which was committed to him in the eternity of his divine pre-existence with the Father.

Both the continuity of the revelatory authority of Christ with that of the Old Testament and its transcendent and ultimate character is pointedly declared by the author of the epistle to the Hebrews: "God, having of old time spoken unto the fathers in the prophets by divers portions and in divers manners, hath at the end of these days spoken unto us in *his* son, whom he appointed heir of all things, through whom also he made the worlds; who being the effulgence of his glory, and the very image of his substance, and upholding all things by the word of his power, when he had made purification of sins, sat down on the right hand of the Majesty on high; having become by so much better than the angels, as he hath inherited a more excellent name than they" (Heb. 1:1-4).

This is the biblical structure of authority in revelation: having spoken in the prophets, God hath spoken in his Son. The many messages given through God's servants lead to the final message spoken by God's Son. But in each case the authority is God's. There is no need for a red-letter Bible.

Also, in each case concrete revelation is given; words are spoken. The speaking of God in the Son is not a dimensionless point in history as so many thinkers after Kierkegaard's "Climacus" have preferred to imagine. The Son speaks the Word as the prophets spoke it; the two phrases, "in the prophets," "in a son" are parallel. The writer of Hebrews goes on to describe the speaking in the Son as the message of a salvation "which having at the first been spoken through the Lord, was confirmed unto us by them that heard; God also bearing witness with them, both by signs and wonders, and by manifold powers, and by gifts of the Holy Spirit, according to his own will" (2:3, 4).

In this passage we have the key to the authority of the message which we preach. It is the authority of one who is the supreme Prophet, and more than a prophet, the divine Son. In that authority, his authority, there is given a message of salvation. This message which was spoken through the Lord has been confirmed to us by those who heard, and their witness has been authenticated by God's miracle-working power.

The words of Jesus are not a fallible human witness to the divine word; rather "the words that I have spoken unto you are spirit, and are life" (John 6:63b). In the Old Testament there is no antithesis between the creative word of power in redemption and the covenantal instruction in the law of God; so also in the Gospels, Jesus speaks the word of life not only when he commands, "Lazarus, come forth," but when he declares, "I am the resurrection, and the life" (John 11:43, 25). He can say, with equal power, "Thy sins are forgiven," or "Arise, and take up thy bed, and walk" (Mark 2:9). The risen Lord not only opens the Scriptures, but commands the apostles to "make disciples of all the nations . . . teaching them to observe all things whatsoever I commanded you" (Matt. 28:19, 20). There is no discipleship without submission to the *torah* of the Messiah.

The gospel has content. It proclaims with authority the

fulfillment of all the covenant promises and the new commandment of the covenant Lord.

Authority in New Testament Terms for Preaching

The principal New Testament terms for the message: *kerygma, evangelion, marturia, didache* all reflect the element of authority. The *kerygma* is the message of the *keryx*, the herald of the King. The term is used in the New Testament of the preaching of Jonah, John the Baptist, Jesus, and the apostles.[43] In each case there is a divine commission, and Jesus stands in the center, who is greater than Jonah, whose sandal-strap John the Baptist was unworthy to loosen, who is the Lord of the apostles. The great announcement is the coming of the kingdom, with the demand which this makes first upon the people of God, and ultimately upon the whole world. The God-centered content of the message requires the official form. Directly and immediately the saving work of God is proclaimed.

There is no less authority in the term *evangelion*. The noun is used by Matthew and Mark, but Luke's use of the verb form is particularly significant. The passage in Luke 4 has already been referred to. This defines the evangel in terms of the prophecy of Isaiah (61:1, 2). That which is fulfilled in the ears of the Nazarenes is the coming in of the great year of jubilee, the climactic era of redemption from bondage, and restoration to the inheritance of grace (Lev. 25:8-17). This helps us to understand why the evangel is first heard in Luke's gospel from the lips of angels. "Good tidings of great joy" — it is *the* good news of the prophets. The kingdom has come because the King has come; salvation has appeared because Christ the Saviour is born. Luke speaks of "evangelizing" the kingdom where others speak of heralding the kingdom. The terms are basically synonymous as the Luke 4 passage shows. The herald's trumpet, like the priest's of old, announces the good news of jubilee (Lev. 25:9).

43. Cf. Matt. 12:41; Luke 11:32; Matt. 3:1; Mark 1:4, 7; Luke 3:3; 4:18, 19; 8:1; Matt. 10:7, 27; I Tim. 2:7; II Tim. 1:11.

In the use of *martureo* and *marturia* we find the same emphasis on authority and again the Old Testament furnishes the background. This element is neglected today in the concept of "witnessing" held by fundamentalists on the one hand and the neo-orthodox on the other. Fundamentalism is heir to many of the weaknesses as well as the strengths of pietism, and conceives of witness in a most subjective sense. One's "testimony" is a recital of one's personal religious experience. Neo-orthodoxy has developed a different kind of subjectivism. Witnesses are "pointers" to the Christ event.

But the basic usage of *marturia* is objective. It is employed in the strict sense for the witness in legal procedures (Exod. 20:16; Deut. 17:6, 7; 19:15-18; Matt. 18:16), and of historical witness: that which is seen, heard, or known.[44] The religious usage is grounded in the technical; the "courtroom" situation remains vivid when the term is used figuratively. The covenant witness is particularly influential in the biblical concept. In the making of a covenant, witnesses are essential to attest the validity of the engagement against any future misrepresentation or evasion. In the Hittite suzerainty treaties the gods were called as witnesses; so also in the covenant between Jacob and Laban, God is made a witness (Gen. 31:50; cf. I Sam. 12:5). In the covenant of the Lord with Israel, heaven and earth are called as witnesses in a figurative sense (Deut. 4:26), and the people are witnesses to their act (Josh. 24:24). The actuality of the event of a covenant may be memorialized or witnessed by objects: stones or pillars (Gen. 31:48; cf. 28:18; Exod. 24:4; Josh. 24:27). The great witness to the covenant, the seal of its objectivity, is the covenant document itself: "Take this book of the law, and put it by the side of the ark of the covenant of Jehovah your God, that it may be there for a witness against thee" (Deut. 31:26). The covenant ordinances are "testimonies" and the term is therefore applied to the ark and the tabernacle as containing these covenant

44. John 4:39; cf. 15:27; I John 1:1; Acts 1:22; 10:41; 6:3; 10:22; 16:2; I Tim. 5:10; III John 6. Cf. also Acts 26:5; Mark 14:55-59; Luke 22:71.

witnesses (Exod. 25:21, 22; 32:15; 38:21; etc.). In his recorded Word, God himself bears constant witness to his covenant.

When, in the prophets, the Lord conducts a covenant controversy with his people, charging them with breach of covenant (Isa. 1:2, 3; 3:13-15; Jer. 2:12; 25:31; Hos. 4:1; 12:2; Mic. 6:1-8),[45] he bears witness against them (Jer. 29:23; Mic. 1:2). On the other hand, the redeemed are witnesses of God's covenant faithfulness in the assembly of the peoples (Isa. 43:10, 12; 44:8), and the Servant of the Lord is the supreme witness (Isa. 43:10; 55:4).

In the gospel the fulfillment of the covenant promise is the object of the witness. God himself is the great Witness. In the Scriptures the Father witnesses to the Son (John 5:37-39); this witness is confirmed by the Spirit and the word spoken from heaven (Luke 3:21, 22; 9:35; John 12:28), and by the words and deeds given to the son (John 5:36). Christ is "the faithful witness" (Rev. 1:5). Just as the *kerygma* and the evangel of covenant realization are declared by him and fulfilled in him, so the witness of covenant attestation is sealed in him. His witness is true, for he declares the heavenly things which he knows and has seen (John 3:11, 12; 8:14, 26; 18:37). The Spirit bears witness of Christ (I John 5:7; John 15:26). The whole record of Pentecost powerfully manifests the work of the Spirit as essential to the apostolic witness.

The witness of the apostles must be understood in connection with the witness of God to and through the Son. The apostolic witness involves testimony to the ministry and miracles of Christ, to the facts of his death and resurrection, as the fulfillment of the covenant. This involves an illuminated understanding of the witness of Scripture to Christ and of the Son's witness to the Father. The apostolic witness therefore is not a narrow recital of one redemptive event. It is broad and deep, setting forth the whole counsel of God. As John tells us, Jesus promised the Spirit, not only to bring to the remembrance of the apostles all that he said to them

45. Cf. H. B. Huffmon, "The Covenant Lawsuit in the Prophets," *Journal of Biblical Literature*, LXXVII, 285ff.

but also to teach them all things (14:26) and to guide them into all the truth (16:13). This wide and profound teaching of the apostles is not secondary; it is not theological speculation occasioned by the great events which they witnessed. It is part of their witness. As "scribes" sent by Christ they bring forth out of the treasury of their illumined understanding things new and old (Matt. 13:52; 23:34). Luke as well as John emphasizes this fact. As we have seen, his summary of the post-resurrection teaching of Jesus in Luke 24:44-49 not only refers to the words that Jesus spoke to the apostles while he was yet with them, but connects these words with the fulfillment of the Old Covenant. Jesus taught that "all things must needs be fulfilled, which are written in the law of Moses, and the prophets, and the psalms, concerning me. Then opened he their mind, that they might understand the scriptures" (vv. 44-45).

This passage concludes, "Ye are witnesses of these things." The apostles are charged to tarry at Jerusalem until they are clothed with power from on high. The witnessing of the apostles described in the book of Acts directly reflects this whole passage.

Matthew, after telling of the resurrection, closes his Gospel with the "Great Commission" in which the total authority of the risen Christ is the explicit basis of the command to make disciples of all the nations, "teaching them to observe all things whatsoever I have commanded you . . ." (Matt. 28:20).

In the New Testament, therefore, as we must expect in the context of covenant law and promise, teaching and witness, we find the closest connection not only between *marturia* and *kerygma,* but also between *marturia* and *didache.* Jesus taught with authority and not as the scribes, and it is the teaching of Jesus, which connects with and fulfills the revelation of the Old Testament, that is to be proclaimed, along with his saving deeds. The apostles working in the power of the Holy Spirit completed those things which Jesus began both to do and to teach as they set forth the meaning of that ministry.

It is a grave mistake to separate, as C. H. Dodd has done, the *kerygma* from the *didache*.[46] In the synagogue of Nazareth Jesus was teacher, herald, and evangelist. The proclamation has the content of the fullness of the counsel of God.

As the word proclaimed from Sinai with the sound of trumpets was to be taught to the people, so the proclamation of the jubilee in Nazareth is to be taught to the nations. Redemptive action is sealed with revelation. The herald's cry to prepare the way of the Lord announces the divine Servant whose law will be a light to the Gentiles (Isa. 42:4; 50:10; 51:4, 16). The *didache* is not secondary but part of the proclamation. "Teaching and evangelizing the word of the Lord" is most natural phraseology for the book of Acts (Acts 15:35; cf. 13:16-41; 19:8, 13; 20:24f.; 28:21, 23).

Herman Ridderbos has pointed out that in the New Testament, *kerygma* is also doctrine, and faith also knowledge, insight, wisdom. He adds, "It is a false antithesis to wish to set faith in Jesus Christ who is the Truth over against having a 'particular system of conceptions and insights' as though faith were something wholly other than this."[47]

Such terms as knowledge, truth, word (*logos*), and wisdom are also related to the message and to *didache* in particular. Wisdom (*sophia*) is ascribed to the young Jesus by Luke immediately after the incident of his boyhood study in the

46. Cf. John J. Vincent, "Didactic Kerygma in the Synoptic Gospels," *Scottish Journal of Theology*, X (1957), 262ff.; David M. Stanley, "Didache as a Constitutive Element of the Gospel Form," *The Catholic Biblical Quarterly*, XVII (1955), 336-348; William L. Lane, *Gospel and Commandment: a Study of the Apostolic Kerygma and Didache* (Unpublished thesis for Th.M. degree, Westminster Theological Seminary, Philadelphia, 1956), pp. 24f. The *didache* has been discussed by Philip Carrington, *The Primitive Christian Catechism* (Cambridge: University Press, 1940); E. G. Selwyn, *The First Epistle of St. Peter* (London: Macmillan, 1946), see Essay II, pp. 363-466. See also H. G. Wood, "Didache, Kerugma and Evangelion" in A. J. B. Higgins, ed., *New Testament Essays: Studies in Memory of T. W. Manson, 1893-1958.* (Manchester: Manchester University Press, 1959), pp. 306-314.

47. Herman Ridderbos, *Heilsgeschiedenis en Heilige Schrift* (Kampen, 1955), p. 141.

temple (Luke 2:40, 52). Jesus' teaching was with wisdom, so that the people marveled (Matt. 13:54; cf. Mark 6:2). Wisdom is also promised to the apostles for their witness (Luke 21:15). We have an instance of such wisdom in the preaching of Stephen, who was full of the Spirit and of wisdom (Acts 6:3, 10; cf. ch. 7). Paul relates true spiritual wisdom to the gospel in the well-known passage in I Corinthians 2:6-16. In Ridderbos' study of Paul's preaching of Christ there is a valuable analysis of this text.[48] In showing that Paul is not here describing a Christian gnosticism, Ridderbos emphasizes the point that the wisdom spoken of is no abstract or speculative *gnosis*, but insight into the meaning of the cross of Christ.

Apostolic Authority and Scripture

The authority of the New Testament gospel is majestically summarized in the Mount of Transfiguration. The voice from the cloud testifies to the final authority of the incarnate Son. Moses, who wrote of him, and Elijah, who prepared the way before him, speak of his coming Exodus at Jerusalem. Their work is done, yet the time has not come for the feast of tabernacles on the mount. They return with the cloud. We have their witness; if we will not receive it, neither will we hear Christ's words (John 5:45-47). But Peter, James, and John remain. Their apostolic ministry is the foundation of authority in the New Testament church, for by their witness the word of Christ is given to the church. As Moses and the prophets witnessed to the coming Redeemer, so the apostles and prophets of the New Testament attest his finished work.[49] Their position is unique. Jesus did not only bear

48. *Paul and Jesus*, trans. D. H. Freeman (Philadelphia: Presbyterian and Reformed Publishing Co., 1957), pp. 56-59.

49. For the immense significance of the apostolate in the New Testament, see the writings of Herman Ridderbos, especially the following: *De Komst van het Koninkrijk* (Kampen: Kok, 1950), pp. 308-336. *De Apostolische Kerk* (Kampen: Kok, 1954), pp. 39-97. *Heilsgeschedenis en Heilige Schrift*, pp. 34-40.

all authority in himself. He also called into being the formal
institution from which all future preaching of the gospel
derives its origin and norm. The apostolate is the link between Christ and his church and fills a most important place
in redemptive history.

When God raised Jesus from the dead, declared Peter,
he gave him to be made manifest, "not to all the people, but
unto witnesses that were chosen before of God, *even* to us,
who ate and drank with him after he rose from the dead"
(Acts 10:41).

In the great saving work of God the election of the apostles
is an essential part. They are chosen to provide the inspired
witness which is definitive for the church. They are not
merely recipients of revelation, but organs of revelation. The
Spirit will bring to their minds that which they have heard,
and teach them all things. Others are given gifts to share
with them in the work, even in the work of mediating revelation (the New Testament prophets also were inspired), but
the apsotles are chosen by Christ himself to deliver, and to
guide in the deliverance of, the whole message to the church.
The picture immediately following Pentecost is valid for
the whole true Christian church: "And they continued sted-
fastly in the apostles' teaching and fellowship . . ." (Acts
2:42).

The apostolic authority is plain in both the oral teaching
and in the fixed form of that authoritative teaching in the
written Scripture. Ridderbos refers to I Corinthians 15 as an
instance of the deliberate inscripturation in the fullness of
apostolic authority of the tradition which the apostles delivered. Thus the deposit of the gospel is committed to the
church. The words of salvation spoken by the Lord are
confirmed unto us by them that heard. A consistent doctrine
of Scripture is maintained in both Testaments; against the
background of the biblical view of revelation it is not in
the least arbitrary, but rather necessary. Inscripturation is
a part and a necessary part of redemptive history.

The Authority of Preaching

As we preach the Word of God we are not clothed in apostolic authority. We cannot bear their eyewitness to the risen Christ. But by God's grace we are numbered among those faithful men into whose hands the apostolic deposit has been placed. Like Timothy we must guard that good deposit through the Holy Spirit who dwelleth in us (II Tim. 1:14). We do so when we hold to the outline of sound words which we read in that Book which contains the witness of the apostles and is the Word of God.

The authority of preaching is not heightened but lost if the preacher forsakes his place behind the Book. We are called to be Christ's but not Christs. The Incarnation is not continued in us, so that we may declare "I say unto you." Nor are we apostles or prophets, inspired of the Spirit to lay afresh the foundations of the church for a new day. We are ministers of the Word; by God's grace wise men and scribes sent by Christ (Matt. 23:34); evangelists, pastors, and teachers; men of God thoroughly furnished by the Holy Scriptures for every good work of our calling. A fitting response to the attacks on a "paper pope" is a deeper study of the written Word of God, a study that will again show us its awesome authority. We bear in our hands the words which Moses carried on the tables of stone down the thundering mountain from the place where angels of God attended the dread theophany. We bear more. We bear the whole witness of the Father to the Son: those things that are written in the law of Moses, and the Prophets, and the Psalms concerning him. In our hands we hold the inspired *kerygma* and *didache* of the witnesses who testify of Christ.

"For if the word spoken through angels proved stedfast, and every transgression and disobedience received a just recompense of reward; how shall we escape, if we neglect so great a salvation? which having at the first been spoken through the Lord, was confirmed unto us by them that heard; God also bearing witness with them, both by signs and wonders, and by manifold powers, and by gifts of the Holy Spirit, according to his own will" (Heb. 2:2-4).

For we do not merely hold this Book in our hands. We have been made stewards of the mysteries of God. There is one requirement for the steward — that he be found faithful. God is faithful who has called us; he gives his Holy Spirit to them that ask him, and it is in the Spirit that we have been set apart to our holy calling. One great gift of the Spirit we must seek in prevailing prayer: that he might open our minds to understand the' Scriptures.

Then our speech and our preaching will not be in persuasive words of wisdom, but in demonstration of the Spirit and of power; for to us also it is given to proclaim the testimony of God.

CHAPTER THREE

BIBLICAL THEOLOGY AND THE CHARACTER OF PREACHING

WITHOUT AUTHORITY preaching is denatured, but authority, even understood in terms of biblical theology, is not the whole of preaching. Other characteristic aspects of the ministry of the Word are renewed through the understanding of redemptive history.

One such insight is to be found in what we may call the perspective of preaching. We proclaim the fullness of the authority of the gospel in a new situation, a situation which the study of biblical theology has helped us to appreciate.

We see Simon Peter standing before the assembled Sanhedrin, Peter the fisherman before the learned and powerful rulers of his nation. It is not the mocking glance of a maidservant that now faces him, or the eyes of slaves and soldiers gleaming in the darkness beside a charcoal fire.

No, Peter who was a coward in the courtyard now stands before the court. Annas, Caiaphas the high priest, Sadducees in rich clothing, contemptuous Pharisees, the learned Gamaliel — Peter sees them circled about on their benches of authority. Hate is in the voice of the high priest: "We strictly charged you not to teach in this name: and behold, ye have filled Jerusalem with your teaching, and intend to bring this man's blood upon us!"

"Oh, no, reverend sir! We intended no such thing; we make no such accusations. We did not realize the seriousness of the situation. We fully recognize your lawful authority. If we could be permitted to withdraw to Galilee . . . we assure you there will be no further disobedience on our part . . . ."

Why did not Peter respond in such a way? How could

such boldness be possible as we hear in the answer that he gave? "We must obey God rather than men. The God of our fathers raised up Jesus, whom ye slew, hanging him on a tree. Him did God exalt with his right hand *to be* a Prince and a Saviour, to give repentance to Israel, and remission of sins. And we are witnesses of these things; and *so is* the Holy Spirit, whom God hath given to them that obey him" (Acts 5:29b-32).

Many insufficient reasons have been offered for Peter's boldness. Peter was certainly not demonstrating a human capacity to do better when given a second chance. Neither is the full explanation in Peter's penitent grief after the cock-crowing, and in his forgiveness by the risen Christ.

The Time in Which We Preach

There is a more specific ground for boldness evident in Peter's own words. It is the totally new perspective that Peter has which rings from every sentence. He stands in a new situation. It is not simply that Peter is different. Everything is different. Peter's witness is to the Triune God whose plan of salvation has been fulfilled in the resurrection and ascension of his Christ.

He witnesses, first, to God the Father who exalted Jesus. The sovereign power of God has been manifested. The opposition of the Sadducees and the whole Sanhedrin is useless. They lifted Jesus to a cross, but God has lifted him to the throne of heaven. The thought of Psalm 110, referred to by Jesus himself and prominent in the apostolic *kerygma*, is present here. The power of the Father establishes the kingdom of the Son. "Sit thou at my right hand, until I make thine enemies thy footstool." The precise language here throws even greater emphasis on God's power. This deed has been wrought *by* God's right hand.[1] Psalm 118, the song of

---

1. *Te dexia* is an instrumental dative. The Septuagint version of Psalm 110:1 (109:1) has *ek dexion*. In Acts 2:33 the dative is used in reporting Peter's words while the Septuagint is followed in the quotation of the Psalm (v. 34). The difference in form seems to be

the Triumphal Entry, has found its fulfillment: "The right hand of Jehovah doeth valiantly. The right hand of Jehovah is exalted . . ." (vv. 15, 16). "The stone which the builders rejected is become the head of the corner. This is Jehovah's doing; it is marvellous in our eyes. This is the day which Jehovah hath made; we will rejoice and be glad in it" (vv. 22-25).

Peter's new orientation is not due merely to a new realization of the power of God and his accountability to God. There has been a new, indeed *the* new, manifestation of that power. We must obey God, for we have seen his right hand exalted in power.

At one with Peter's consciousness of the power of God in the exaltation of Christ is his understanding of the saving purpose of God in that exaltation. It is impossible for us to imagine the sense of utter shock, the total dismay which engulfed the disciples at the crucifixion of Jesus Christ. For Peter this experience must have been extreme indeed. It must be remembered that the ties which bound Simon Peter to Jesus were no mere ties of friendship and love. It was a religious bond that linked Peter with his Saviour. When all were forsaking Jesus, Simon Peter had confessed him as the very Son of God. How could the Prince of Life be murdered? How could the Son of God be dead? Yet the very depths of that despair prepared the way for Peter's new understanding of the culmination of the saving purposes of God. Not only had death been swallowed up in victory; in the light of his new understanding, with his eyes opened to perceive the Scriptures, Peter recognized that the death itself was part of the victory. He understood that according to the Scriptures, Christ must needs suffer and enter into his glory. Repeatedly in the book of Acts we find the evidence of Peter's revering recognition of the fulfillment of these pur-

---

deliberate and there is no reason to depart from the usual force of the dative, especially since the language of Psalm 118:16, referred to in connection with the Triumphal Entry, forms a background for the idea of the exaltation taking place through the power of God's right hand.

poses of God: "But the things which God foreshowed by the mouth of all the prophets, that his Christ should suffer, he thus fulfilled" (Acts 3:18). Christ was delivered up by the "determinate counsel and foreknowledge of God" (Acts 2:23).

This same new perspective appears in Peter's witness to the sovereignty of the Christ as Saviour in his exaltation. He sees him exalted as a Prince. In divine Messianic glory he is over his own and over all the world. The terms Prince and Saviour fall naturally together. In the Old Testament background the term "saviour" is a kingly title. In its ultimate force it marks the salvation of God himself. Peter is confessing that Christ on the throne is the Lord of salvation. He who is mighty to save gives to Israel the gifts of his exaltation: repentance and remission of sins. Sovereign and gracious gifts these, gifts which could come only from God.

Knowledge of the power and the saving purpose of his ascended Lord casts fear out of the heart of Simon Peter. The glance of the Saviour in his sufferings had moved Peter from oaths of denial to tears of penitence, but now the witness of the Spirit to the glory of that same Saviour on the throne of heaven lifts Peter to the holy boldness of a witness. We sense that just as Stephen looked up to heaven as he rendered the supreme *marturia*, and saw the glorified Christ at the right hand of God, so Peter, too, looks up with the eye of faith, recognizing that he stands in the new age, the time of fulfillment, the time of the coming in of the kingdom of God with power. The evidence of that power is all about him and within him. He stands with the twelve; the apostolic witnesses of the new Israel confront the apostate judges of the old. They have been made witnesses through the reality of Christ's exaltation. Because he is enthroned at the right hand of God, he has sent forth the Holy Spirit into their hearts. "We are witnesses of these things and so is the Holy Spirit whom God hath given to them that obey him."

Our preaching cannot have the boldness or the urgency of

Peter's until we have understood the perspective from which his addresses are formed, the perspective of the whole New Testament. Biblical theology has here rendered a great service to the church. On all sides it is recognized that any who would take the New Testament seriously must be confronted by eschatology. Peter's witness must search the soul of every preacher. If a man cannot believe in Christ's ascension, he cannot preach the apostolic gospel or know the power of Pentecost. For Peter, Christ's heavenly rule is no more a myth than was his crucifixion. It will not do to reject Peter's witness and then to seek some noble truth unconsciously symbolized in Peter's mistaken conviction. Such sophisticated unbelief can never know the bold urgency of Christian preaching. It is painful to hear a man who does not believe Peter's gospel seeking to preach as though, in some sense, he did. Yet it is even more painful to hear a man, who does believe Peter's gospel, preaching as though he did not. Preaching that has lost urgency and passion reveals a loss of the eschatological perspective of the New Testament. Such a preacher does not stand before the Prince of salvation as Peter did. He is not aware that he ministers in the time of the ascended Christ, the time of the fulfillment of all the prophets in his saving rule.

The New Testament recognizes that we are living in the latter days. The prophetic view of history is divided into the former days and the latter days and the point of division is the coming of the Messiah. "God . . . hath *at the end of these days* spoken unto us in his Son" (Heb. 1:1-2, italics added).

The joy of the Christian gospel stems from the recognition of this fact. The evangel of the prophet Isaiah is that which is fulfilled by Jesus of Nazareth. The year of jubilee has come, therefore we must proclaim liberty to the captive. This is the reason for the marvelous fact that Peter, on trial for his life, nevertheless evangelizes. He does not threaten the judgment and destruction of those men who crucified Christ and are threatening to crucify him. The day of their judgment will come. But Christ has been exalted as a Prince and a Saviour to give *repentance* to Israel and *remission* of sins. It is the sovereign Saviour that Peter preaches. Our great sin in preaching is our little faith and therefore our little joy. We forget who our Saviour is and where he is. We even manage to preach christology without any real understanding of the present kingship of Christ. We need to cry with Peter, "Repent ye therefore, and turn again, that your sins may be blotted out, that so there may come seasons of refreshing from the presence of the Lord; and that he may send the Christ who hath been appointed for you, *even* Jesus: whom the heaven must receive until the times of restoration of all things, whereof God spake by the mouth of his holy prophets that have been from of old" (Acts 3:19-21).

The force of Peter's perspective is revealed in that passage. The latter days have come, the days in which the Lord is glorified, and he has poured out his Spirit upon men. But it is not yet the time of the restoration of all things. The glorified Lord is also a coming Lord. It is the end time but it is also the interim time — the days between his first and second coming.

The joy of his resurrection, the power of his Spirit, the hope of his coming — preaching oriented in this perspective honors Christ.

The Place in Which We Preach

There is another aspect to the perspective of our preaching. We might say that it is not merely the time in which we preach but the place in which we preach. Our Lord has gone to glory, but we are not with him in his victorious rule. We are in the world as his witnesses, and we are in the world so that we may be his witnesses. In J. H. Bavinck's *An Introduction to the Science of Missions*, a book which makes excellent use of the insights of biblical theology, there is a vivid page which describes how the Lord launched the church almost in spite of itself on its world-wide mission.[2] It now seems almost incredible that with the book of Acts in the Scriptures the church could ever have lost sight of its mission. No doubt this came about through the confusion of the church and the state which began in the age of Constantine. It was justified theologically by a misconstruction of biblical theology. It was assumed that the task of carrying the gospel to the whole world had been given to the apostles alone, and that with the end of the apostolic office this aspect of the church's calling disappeared. That this is poor theology should be evident from the great passage at the close of Matthew's gospel. Christ's promise that he will be with the church to the end of the age in the discharge of its task plainly shows that the work cannot be limited to the apostles. The gospel message as it is defined in the New Testament is a missionary message which concerns the whole world. He who does not see the need of proclaiming it does not understand it.

The whole world, then, is the place where the gospel must be preached. It is also true that the place of preaching is in the church. Biblical-theological studies have brought a fresh recognition of the position the church occupies in the teaching of Jesus. Paul not only preached in the market place at Athens, he also engaged in familiar discourse with the Christians assembled in the upper room at Troas.

Biblical theology will aid us in relating these two areas of the perspective of preaching. As we have seen, C. H. Dodd separates radically the original *kerygma* from the secondary *didache*. It has been said that preaching in the church is not strictly *kerygma* at all. Dahl has suggested that "putting in remembrance" is a better term.[3] Now it cannot be denied

---

2. J. H. Bavinck, *Inleiding in de Zendingswetenschap* (Kampen, 1954), p. 48; trans. by David H. Freeman, *An Introduction to the Science of Missions* (Philadelphia: Presbyterian and Reformed Publishing Co., 1960), pp. 37f.

3. Nils A. Dahl, *"Anamnesis.* Mémoire et Commémoration dans le christianisme primitif," *Studia Theologica* I (Lund, 1948), pp. 69-95. Cf. Herman Ridderbos, *Heilsgeschiedenis en Heilige Schrift,* pp. 134f.

that when the gospel is being made known to those who have never heard it, it is presented differently than when it is being preached to those who have been instructed in the truth from childhood. Even in preaching to Christians there is milk for the babes in Christ and strong meat for those who have their spiritual faculties exercised (I Cor. 3:1, 2; Heb. 5:11-14). The wisdom of God which Paul proclaimed among the full-grown could not be presented to the spiritually immature (I Cor. 2:6).

However, there is great danger in losing sight of either aspect of the perspective of the place of preaching. The gospel must always be preached in the church and in the world. *Kerygma, evangelion, didache, marturia*: all these and other terms for the content of the gospel are used with great flexibility in the New Testament. *Kerygma* is used as an inclusive term and not merely for missionary preaching. Paul's use of it in his charge to Timothy (II Tim. 4:2) is very broad. Heralding the Word is linked with reproving, rebuking, and exhorting with all longsuffering and teaching. Timothy fulfills the work of an *evangelist* by teaching sound doctrine. The conclusion of the Epistle to the Romans is a grand illustration of the way in which Paul regards the *kerygma* as including the proclamation of the whole counsel of God (Rom. 16:25-27). At the beginning of the same epistle Paul speaks of evangelizing those to whom he writes (Rom. 1:15). In Acts 5:42 we read that "every day, in the temple and at home," the apostles "ceased not to teach and to preach Jesus as the Christ." Both teaching and preaching are involved in winning men to Christ and in building up believers.

It is true that there were both teachers and evangelists in the New Testament church. Yet these are co-laborers in the gospel and ministers of the Word. As Ridderbos has pointed out in discussing the alleged "gnosis" passage in I Corinthians 2, Paul's teaching of wisdom was centered in the cross.[4] An evangelist who did not teach would be no evange-

---

4. Herman Ridderbos, *Paul and Jesus*, pp. 56-59.

list in the New Testament pattern. He would have no resemblance to Timothy or Philip. On the other hand, a teacher who forgot that his message is the eternal *evangel* could never build up the church in knowing Christ, the power of his resurrection, and the fellowship of his suffering. The teacher of the church must prepare "children of God without blemish in the midst of a crooked and perverse generation, among whom ye are seen as lights in the world, holding forth the word of life" (Phil. 2:15b, 16a).

The Holy Spirit who indwells those who have obeyed him is a witness to Christ. They who walk in the Spirit therefore must shine as lights in the world. The witness of Jesus is the spirit of prophecy. The whole Bible testifies of him. We have been given that Word in order that we might make it known. The church is not the consummation kingdom but it presses toward the consummation. The church must always be a pilgrim church hastening on toward the end of time and the ends of the earth.[5] To be sure, missions cannot be made the only function of the church, so that the church is defined by its "apostolate."[6] This view misunderstands the character of the apostolate and it also denies in effect the particularism of salvation. However, in rejecting

5. Lesslie Newbigin, *The Household of God* (London: S. C. M. Press, 1953), p. 132.

6. This viewpoint is vigorously advocated by J. C. Hoekendijk, "The Church in Missionary Thinking," *The International Review of Missions,* XLI (1952), 333f. "The *nature* of the Church can be sufficiently defined by its *function,* i.e. its participation in Christ's apostolic ministry" (p. 334). Cf. also Hendrik Kraemer, *The Christian Message in a Non-Christian World* (New York: Harper, 1938), p. 2: "The essential nature of the Church is that it is an *apostolic* body. It is this, not because its authority is derived from the apostles, for the apostles belong to the Church, but because in all its words and actions it ought to be a bearer of witness to God and His decisive creative and redeeming acts and purposes." For discussions of this question see A. A. Van Ruler, *Theologie van het Apostolaat* (Nijkerk: Callenbach, 1954), especially pp. 35ff.; Lesslie Newbigin, *The Household of God,* pp. 147f.; G. Brillenburg Wurth, " 'Het Apostolaat van de Kerk' in Deze Tijd," J. Ridderbos *et al., De Apostolische Kerk,* pp. 98-133.

such a view, we must be most careful that we do not deny the apostolicity of the church. For the church is founded upon the apostles and the prophets. The message which it has received from them is the witness to Christ crucified, risen, and ascended. The worship of the church is an end in itself, not simply a means to evangelism. The growth in grace of the church in which it is built up in Christ is also an end in itself to the glory of God. But if the witness of the church is forgotten or muffled there can be no growth through true edification, and our worship will not be pleasing to our God who is to be adored by that vast company from every kindred and tongue and people and nation.

In my judgment, it is a mistake to divide between homiletics and evangelistic preaching ("halieutics") as two distinct areas of study. In the Netherlands both Hoekstra and Dijk have done this, following Abraham Kuyper's *Encyclopaedie.*[7] It is easy, of course, to point to extreme differences in technique

7. Abraham Kuyper, *Encyclopaedie der Heilige Godgeleerheid,* III, 488: "The Kerygma with which the church comes to the *unbelievers,* is so wholly something other than the homily in the midst of the *believers,* that it would be illogical to wish to join the technical theory for both under one concept." Kuyper urges this objection against combining homiletics and "evangelistics" in a broader discipline called "keryktics." In his organization, the teaching disciplines are: homiletics, catechetics, liturgics, and "prosthetics" (he prefers this term to halieutics and others for the science of missions). Hoekstra in his *Gereformeerde Homiletiek* follows Kuyper's division, but divides "prosthetics" into theory of missions and theory of evangelism — "evangelistics" (p. 31). Hoekstra is also emphatic in distinguishing the character of homiletics from that of "mission preaching" or evangelism (e.g. p. 185). His textbook deals with homiletics only, in distinction from these other subjects. The same viewpoint is adopted by Karl Dijk, *De Dienst der Prediking* (Kampen: Kok, 1955), p. 96: "The work of the gospel outside the church is indeed not less a service of Christ through his ministers, and this work outside may in no respect be neglected, but before it there stands the pastoral care of our Saviour for his flock, and in this care the ministry of the Word takes the first place; this ministry is directed to the church of the Lord, and when we here speak of preaching, we mean this diaconia." J. T. Bakker warns against a sharp division in *Kerygma en Prediking* (Kampen: Kok, 1957), pp. 24f.

in preaching to tribesmen who have never heard the gospel on the one hand, and to a well-indoctrinated church on the other. But the result of the division has been that many young preachers have come to think of themselves as homileticians who have nothing to do with missions. One sometimes gets the impression that a pastor should study homiletics and that an evangelist should study halieutics. Since in the traditional Reformed position the evangelist is an extraordinary officer in the church who disappeared from the scene with the apostolic age, it is perhaps easy to understand why the science of halieutics has not had a comparable development to homiletics. A better course is to see the riches of the gospel in the wide diversity of terms that are used, and to recognize that when we preach that gospel we must preach it in all of its aspects: to *salvation* in the broadest sense of that term. In discussing the problem of tongues in the church at Corinth, Paul argues from the impression made on the outsider who is in attendance at the meeting of the church (I Cor. 14:23-25). The preacher in the pulpit is in the world as well as in the church. He must proclaim the gospel in its fullness.

The Richness of Preaching

This fullness of the gospel is evident not only in the variety of those to whom it is addressed but in the richness of preaching itself. As we have already seen, preaching in the biblical sense cannot be limited to bare proclamation. It is also teaching and it embraces every mode of application from the sternest rebuke to the tenderest entreaty and comfort. Since it is the declaration of God's name it is addressed not only to men, but also to God. It is an act of worship. Our preaching often lacks the punctuation of the exclamation point of praise. Unlike the Scriptures, our sermons are so centered on men that they neglect to bless God. The doxologies that burst from Paul in the midst of his expositions never trouble our placid pools of prose.

Textual preaching has long been advocated as a strong remedy for monochromatic sermons. Without an appreciation of biblical theology, however, even the riot of color in the profusion of Scriptural texts may be tamed by the dark glasses of the preacher. Understanding the place of preaching in the history of redemption will itself bring to the foreground the richness as well as the authority of this service of God. To appreciate the recital of covenant history, the response of the hymn of praise, the reflection of the wise man, the denunciations of the prophet, the epistles of an apostle in the significance of their form as well as their content is to gain a new appreciation of the richness of setting forth God's Word. The more fully a text is approached in the context of its own setting in redemptive history, the better is the preparation for preaching that is not uniformly hortatory, or didactic, or even sentimental, but rather reflects the glory of the Word.

Preaching Christ

Most important of all, biblical theology serves to center preaching on its essential message: Jesus Christ. Preaching must be theological. Salvation is of the Lord, and the message of the gospel is the theocentric message of the unfolding of the plan of God for our salvation in Jesus Christ. He who would preach the Word must preach Christ. Yet even where this principle has long been acknowledged, the practice of preaching often falls far short of this ideal. "There is still so much, forgive me the words, twisted and bungled [preaching]. One hears sermons in which the name of Christ is not named except toward the end in an applicatory conclusion. Another preacher feels burdened from the beginning to set the work of Christ in the center because he actually thinks that the text says nothing of it."[8] It is here that the biblical-theological approach will open the way to resolving our difficulties. The unifying structure of Scripture is the struc-

8. F. W. Grosheide, *De Eenheid der Nieuw-Testamentische Gods-openbaring* (Kampen, 1918), p. 33. Quoted in T. Hoekstra, *op. cit.*, p. 173.

ture of redemptive history. The Bible does not have the form of a textbook, and the witness to Christ unfolds with the progressive epochs of revelation which in turn are grounded in the successive periods of redemption. Biblical theology recognizes both the unity and the epochal structure of redemptive history. As we progress in our study of each period in its own context and "theological horizon," if we may so speak, we discover that each epoch has a coherent and organic structure and also that there is organic progression from period to period as the plan of God is revealed.

In no other way can we make our preaching genuinely theological and christocentric. Without insight into the theological horizon of the period concerned, we will fall into thin moralizing which misses the progress of redemptive history and fails to see Christ in the midst. Abraham's sacrifice of Isaac will be only the supreme testing of a great man's faith. Or, in avoiding that error, we may seize upon an artificial connection and introduce Christ into the passage by sheer force of allegory. Lesser preachers than Origen have attempted that solution, and have desperately clutched at the red cord hanging from Rahab's window as a type of the blood of Christ.

If, on the other hand, we develop the most thorough knowledge of the period without relating its conceptions to the whole structure of redemptive history, we may risk the mistake of the history of religions school, failing to recognize, in the organic development of the whole, the hand of God in redemption and his voice in revelation. The Christian proclamation of an Old Testament text is not the preaching of an Old Testament sermon.

Many sermons on the revelation of the covenant name of God in Exodus 3 have lacked biblical-theological depth altogether. The preacher has fortified himself with studies of the etymology of the *tetragrammaton* and has studied carefully the locus of theology proper with respect to the divine being. He may even have indulged in some philosophical and theological reflection. But of the setting in God's redemptive history he seems altogether unaware. The "I am" God he preaches simply as "l'Eternel," not as the God of self-determined grace who takes the sovereign initiative in redeeming his people and who cannot be moved from his faithfulness to his promises.

However, even when the preacher has a clear conception of the significance of this revelation in its setting, there may be a failure to see the total relationship which it bears to God's whole work of redemption and revelation. One may thereby fail to relate the name of Jehovah to the name of Jesus in which it is fulfilled.

To discover Christ in the Scriptures no desperate allegories are necessary, although the mind of faith is. The hearts of the disciples on the road to Emmaus burned within them as Christ opened the Scriptures. They were not in the least amazed at his cleverness, but only at their dullness in not having perceived long ago the sufferings and glory of Christ so clearly set forth.

The revelation of Christ is in accord with the nature of the Redeemer and the redeemed. Because Christ is the eternal *Logos*, God the Son, in every revelation of God *he* also is revealed. When we read the Genesis account of creation we learn of him, for "all things were made by him, and without him was not anything made that was made." No doubt John intends that we should understand a more pointed allusion to Christ in the record than in the mere fact that God is spoken of. The objectifying of the word of God in the Old Testament, and the act of creation by the word provides an indication of the mystery of the Trinity. So also, while the progress of God's self-revelation in the Old Testament invariably points toward the fullness of that revelation in Christ, there are in the course of that revelation more explicit indications of the Second Person of the Trinity. Expressed in terms of the covenant, this means that Christ is the Lord, and in whatever way we learn of the Lord we learn of him. But the Covenant Lord comes to his people, dwells in their midst, and promises a final deliverance, an ultimate covenant of peace to be established by his coming. Since it is the Son of God who fulfills these promises, the redemptive epiphanies of God are particular revelations of Christ. When the Lord descends on Sinai, marches through the desert, and ascends Zion, leading captivity captive (the dramatic description of Psalm 68), this redemptive appearance manifests the saving action that will find its culmination in Christ (cf. Eph. 4:8, Ps. 68:18).

But precisely because the coming of the Lord to his people, his dwelling in their midst, is carried to the ultimate reach of the incarnation, Christ is identified with the people as well as with their God. He who is the Lord becomes the Servant. The eternal Son is born of Mary to bring many sons to glory. This accounts for the other principal mode by which Christ is manifested in the Old Testament. God's calling of his people, his dwelling with them, can be realized only in Christ; therefore the status and role of the covenant servant bears constant testimony to Christ. Put in filial terms, with which the covenantal figure is closely associated, Christ is the promised Seed, the Son of the woman, and where that Seed is manifested, Christ is in view.

Again, though in quite another way, there is a further specification of Christ's work. The mediatorial role in which men approach God on behalf of the people manifests the servant of the Lord, the man of God in a special sense. Moses as the mediator of the covenant thus prefigures Christ, and is the servant figure in the background of the Messianic Servant prophecies in Isaiah. The other official servants of God, prophets, priests, kings, are the anointed who manifest the calling of the Messiah.

All the many detailed prophecies of Christ which stud the pages of the Old Testament are related to this fundamental structure of salvation. Through the method of biblical theology the redemptive significance of a particular revelation in a particular period is studied and seen in the perspective which converges on Christ.

The Redemptive and the Ethical

Biblical theology, then, serves to unlock the objective significance of the history of salvation. It focuses on the core of redemptive history in Christ. On the other hand it also opens up for us the subjective aspect, the religious riches of the *experience* of God's people, and its relation to our own.

This statement may appear dubious, for the history of redemption and individual religious experience have often been set over against each other. Those who have championed the preaching of the history of salvation (*Heilsgeschichte*) have attacked "moralizing."[9] It has been assumed by some that a choice must be made between ethical preaching and that which is redemptive-historical. The New Testament, however, not only sanctions both but does not set them in opposition. The use which James makes of the histories of Job and of Elijah is a clear instance of the deriving of ethical instruction from Old Testament history (Jas. 5:11, 17). So also in I Corinthians 10:11 Paul declares, "Now these things happened unto them by way of example; and they were written for our admonition, upon whom the ends of the ages are come." The ethical force of Old Testament history could not be more strongly stated; but as B. Holwerda has pointed out, the phrase "upon whom the ends of the ages are come" reveals

9. In the Netherlands, the late B. Holwerda criticized moralistic preaching and was misunderstood as denying the ethical application of Scripture. His contention was, however, that only by the redemptive-historical method could the meaning of the text be grasped and a sound application achieved. See "De Heilshistorie in de Prediking," in ". . . *Begonnen Hebbende van Mozes* . . ." (Terneuzen: D. H. Littooij, 1953), pp. 79-118.

Karl Dijk, while critical of Holwerda's approach (he fears an artificial attempt to plot the development of God's revelation as a precise curve), acknowledges that preaching which ignores the *historia revelationis,* which "again and again equates Abraham and us, Moses' struggle and ours, Peter's denial and our unfaithfulness; which proceeds only illustratively, does not bring the Word of God and does not permit the church to see the glory of the work of God; it only preaches man, the sinful, the sought, the redeemed, the pious man, but not Jesus Christ" (*De Dienst der Prediking,* Kampen: 1955, p. 109).

that the perspective is that of the history of redemption.[10] The Israelites are examples, not as an ancient people whose experiences happened to resemble ours in certain respects, but as the people of God, occupying a particular place in the plan of the ages, that is, in the history of redemption. Only in the structure of such an understanding of Israelite history can Paul find the analogies that he does to Christian experience (vv. 1-3) centering in the symbol of the rock as a type of Christ.[11]

We do well, then, to avoid setting up a false antithesis between the redemptive-historical approach and what might

10. Holwerda, *loc. cit.* He further insists that *typos* in the Pauline usage refers to prefiguring rather than merely exemplifying in a general sense.

11. The Old Testament narrative provides a basis for the identification of Christ as the rock that is not always appreciated by those who look upon Paul's statement here as merely rabbinical allegorizing. In Exodus 17:1-7 the whole narrative is structured by the concept of a controversy, "Meribah." See B. Gemser, "The RIB — or Controversy-Pattern in Hebrew Mentality," in M. Noth and D. W. Thomas, eds., *Wisdom in Israel and in the Ancient Near East* (Leiden: E. J. Brill, 1955), pp. 120-137.

The people bring suit against Moses; if their accusation is sustained he is liable to execution by stoning (v. 4). Moses protests that their charge is actually against God, whom they are tempting (v. 2b). They are accusing God of breach of covenant (cf. the Lord's controversy with Israel, Mic. 6:1-8). At the word of the Lord a solemn session of Moses and the elders is convened before the people (v. 5). This is a court scene for the trial. God takes the place of the defendant before the judge (v. 6). As in Deuteronomy 25:1-3, the verdict is pronounced as a "smiting," to be executed in this case by the rod as the symbol of God's judicial authority — "wherewith thou smotest the river" (v. 5). Instead of Israel's being smitten, the rock on which God stands is smitten. The rock is a symbol of deity in the ancient Near East, and is a divine name in the pentateuch (Deut. 32:4, 15, 18, 30, 31). In Psalms which refer to Meribah, this name is used for God (Ps. 78:15, 20, 35; 95:1).

The Exodus passage itself seems to require that we understand a symbolic divine bearing of the judgment, from which the streams of grace flow. Such an interpretation would explain why Moses' unauthorized smiting of the rock a second time was so serious an offense (Num. 20:10-13).

be called an ethical approach to the Scriptures, particularly in the historical passages. The redemptive-historical approach necessarily yields ethical application, which is an essential part of the preaching of the Word. Whenever we are confronted with the saving work of God culminating in Christ, we are faced with ethical demands. A religious response of faith and obedience is required. But that response must be evoked by the truth of the particular revelation which is before us. To understand that truth we must know the context of the revelation in its period. Without this structure biblical history becomes a chaotic jumble, and little in the lives of biblical characters seems either relevant to our lives or worthy of imitation.

Those who find only collected moral tales in the Bible are constantly embarrassed by the *good* deeds of patriarchs, judges, and kings. Surely we cannot pattern our daily conduct on that of Samuel as he hews Agag to pieces, or Samson as he commits suicide, or Jeremiah as he preaches treason. Judged by our usual ethics, Michal was quite right in despising David's performance before the ark, and Judas in criticizing the extravagance of Mary's use of perfume in Bethany. Dreadful consequences have ensued when blindness to the history of revelation was coupled with the courage to follow misunderstood examples. Heretics have been hewed in pieces in the name of Christ, and imprecatory psalms sung on the battlefields.

Yet in the coherence of the history of redemption, none of these patterns is to be rejected, and each has relevance to our situation. Samuel, the prophetic judge, executed the verdict of God's own sentence against Agag (". . . before the Lord in Gilgal," I Sam. 15:33), wielding the sword in a period when God revealed his wrath against the wicked in theocratic war. Such judgment is now committed to Christ, who did not spare himself from the supreme visitation of wrath for sinners, but who also will not spare those who have despised his grace in the day of the wrath of the Lamb. Every temporizing mitigation of the absoluteness of God's judgment is an attack on Calvary as well as on the throne of God, and it is warned by Samuel's act. Christ has not now given the sword but the keys to those who are charged with authority in his name. The sanctifying of God's name in spiritual church discipline reflects in our situation the theocratic obedience of Samuel.

Samson also is a judge and savior of God's people, and his death is not wicked self-destruction but is the price of a victory against the enemies and mockers of God; Jeremiah's "treason" is against a king and people who have forsaken God's covenant; it is actually utter loyalty to the supreme Sovereign; David's exulting joy prefigures the triumph of the ascension of Christ; Mary's extravagant worship anoints the Lord's Anointed before his burial. All these not only testify of Christ but provide a deeper understanding of our own obedience to him. The redemptive-historical may by no means be contrasted with the practical.

Relating the history of redemption to the ethical in the explication of the text does cause problems to arise. Every evangelical preacher has struggled more or less consciously with them, and a teacher of homiletics has many opportunities to observe young men facing them for the first time. Student sermons very often include one of these elements and ignore the other. Occasionally both elements appear, plainly unresolved, but unequally yoked together under a conveniently ambiguous theme.

There is of course no patented solution to this difficulty. To make the first point of the sermon outline "Its doctrinal content" and point two "Its ethical demand" may be patentable, but it is hardly a satisfactory solution. However, it is just here that the development of biblical-theological insight points to the right path.

The solution is the organic relationship that exists in God's great work of redemption and revelation, a relationship that it is the work of biblical theology to study. Just as the ethical response is always required by the covenant of grace, so the ethical is never artificially or inconsequentially present in the lives and actions of those figures who play decisive roles in the history of redemption. Because the work of redemption is one work and the covenant of grace is one covenant the basic relationships are the same. Unbelief on the part of the children of Israel in the wilderness parallels our unbelief, not simply in terms of psychological similarity but in the total structure of redemptive history. We upon whom the ends of the ages are come are a redeemed and pilgrim people led to the promised land by the Lord who dwells among us.

Through the study of the biblical-theological horizon of a period we may interpret the ethical demands of that period in theologically accurate terms. Such interpretation enables us to perceive the relationship of that ethical element to our own situation.

David and Goliath

Let us take an example or two of such an approach. David's slaying of Goliath has often been preached on in such a way as to be merely "illustrative" with a vengeance. Indeed, one hears sermons on this theme that might almost as well have been preached on Jack the Giant Killer. But even when perception rises above the level on which David is seen as a brave shepherd boy who was a dead shot with the sling, the improvement is often merely a stress on David's faith and God's faithfulness in granting him victory. So conceived, this incident slips into a vast store of miscellaneous victories of faith in the Old Testament.

When the biblical-theological dimension is added the story is viewed in a new light. The significance of the kingship in the development of the theocracy must be appreciated, for David is the Lord's anointed. In this incident he is manifested to Israel as a divinely endowed savior of the people. Only in this perspective can David's words to Goliath in I Samuel 17:45-47 be given their proper force. They then become the theological core of the whole passage. David's attack is in the name of Jehovah of hosts, the God of the armies of Israel.

His victory will testify to all the earth that there is a God in Israel. David appears as the restorer of the theocracy from shame to its rightful function as a witness to God's sovereignty to save. Further, his victory is that "all this assembly may know" the futility of carnal weapons and the sovereignty in salvation of the covenant God. Here David is proclaiming as a prophet the deepest principles of the history of salvation, principles which find their fulfillment only in that theocratic King who is David's greater Son. It is impossible not to see Christ in this passage.

However, David is also an actor in the battle. It is by his hand that Goliath is to be slain. Courage is required to go forth against the giant. Yet these two elements fit in perfect harmony. The theological interpretation, the redemptive-historical interpretation, is on David's own lips as he goes into battle. Nor do these words appear as theologizing "dubbed into" the narrative. They are most concrete. David catalogs the sword, the spear, and the javelin with which Goliath approaches him, and he is grimly realistic about the disposal of the dead body of this blaspheming giant.

By the unction of the Spirit, David has insight into his own role in redemptive history. He understands the nature of Israel and the purpose of the existence of this nation. He also understands the nature of the covenant God, his omnipotence, and his faithfulness. Further, he understands his own position as an instrument of the Lord. His power is of the Lord who saves not with sword and spear, for the battle is his. Do we not perceive that David's possession, in a measure, of this insight was necessary to his role in redemptive history? Indeed, is not this the issue in the rejection of Saul and the establishment of the kingdom in David's hands? In David's later testing through the persecution of Saul, it is this principle in his own understanding that is repeatedly challenged by circumstances and embraced by faith. The true theocratic King must be one whose glory is the name of God, who comes not in his own name but in the name of the God who sends him.

The real ethical and religious issues in David's own experience are in perfect congruity with the significance of the redemptive history, for David himself perceives the nature of those issues, and his stature and usefulness in the history of redemption depend upon the fact that he does so. Saul, of course, has a negative role in the history of redemption because of his failure to perceive the issues; but the connection between the ethical and the redemptive-historical is the same.

In connecting our experience with David's we need only to understand that we upon whom the ends of the ages are come are a kingdom of priests and a holy nation. He that is feeble among us is as David, for the house of David is as God, as the angel of Jehovah before us (Zech. 12:8). Each of us has official responsibility to exalt the name of the Lord of hosts before the people of God and the world.

When we thus approach the Scriptures, ready to appreciate the grasp of the "redemptive-historical figures" upon the principles of redemption, we are using a scriptural method. We have only to recall the descriptions of Abraham and Moses in the eleventh chapter of Hebrews to see that this is so. These men were not only actors in the great redemptive-historical movement that culminated in Christ. They themselves looked for Christ, and they possessed this Christian hope not as a bare prophetic enigma but as a living hope, full of meaning for their daily consciousness and experience. It conformed to the deepest realities of their religious life as they hungered and thirsted for God. They saw and greeted the promises from afar. They confessed that they were strangers and pilgrims on earth — even as we, who have here no abiding city — and they desired that heavenly country, that city which hath foundations, whose builder and maker is God.

Abraham's Sacrifice

The test of Abraham is illuminating for us as we consider this problem. At first glance the redemptive-historical and the ethical seem entirely incompatible. On the one hand we have the sheer challenge of Abraham's faith: the command to sacrifice Isaac. On the other hand we have the redemptive-historical picture of the substitutionary atonement on the mount of the Lord. Does Abraham perform his role on an entirely different plane from that of the redemptive-historical movement? Is the human dimension here totally unrelated to the divine? Does God require of Abraham the very contradiction of all righteousness? Is it the surd of the paradoxical religious consciousness, the teleological suspension of the ethical, to use Kierkegaard's phrase, that here appears?

Such questions spring from insufficient grasp of the biblical theology of this period. Abraham's theological horizon must be taken more seriously into account. The initiative of the divine grace with Abraham must be recalled. The covenant relation as one of confirmed promise must be understood. Isaac must be seen not merely as Abraham's son whom he loves, but as his *only* son (Gen. 22:2); not the only son naturally, but the only son before God, the only son of the promise. Isaac, as Abraham well knows, is the seed of the promise: ". . . in Isaac shall thy seed be called" (Gen. 21:12). The command is not a bare command to a certain man to go kill his son. The command is to Abraham to offer up the promised seed as a burnt-offering in a particular place in the land of promise. The seed which God has miraculously given is to be claimed by God's judgment. Yet God cannot be unfaithful who promised. The covenant stands or falls in the seed. Only in and through the offering of the seed of promise is Abraham's worship acceptable to God. *Redemption* is through the seed of the promise, and this is what Abraham seeks. Had he been looking only for an earthly inheritance secure in his tribal descent he would not have left Ur or Haran. Yet, on the other hand, if the promised seed is offered, how can the whole promise come to realization? And how can redemption come through a son who may be justly claimed in the holiness of God's judgment?

Abraham could not fully answer these questions. Yet his faith was not irrational or blind. He saw and greeted the promises from afar. Hear his answer: "God will provide himself the lamb for a burnt-offering, my son." Jehovah-Jireh — in the mount of the Lord it shall be provided!

How eloquently does the name of the altar express the character of Abraham's faith! Through God's provision the promises must be fulfilled! In the mount of the promise the redemption of the people of God would take place by God's own provision. Abraham's seed are the redeemed, and from Abraham's seed must come the Redeemer. The Lord will provide! "Your father Abraham rejoiced to see my day; and he saw it, and was glad" (John 8:5).

Are we reading too much into Abraham's faith? No, I think not. Rather, we are only beginning to understand the setting of that faith in that period of redemption and revelation in which it was required of Abraham. We are only beginning to see the meaning of the principle of the redemption of the first-born which applied not only to Abraham, but to all the people of God in the passover ordinance (Exod. 13:11-15), and in the consecration of the Levites (together with the payment of the five shekels for those who were additional to the number of the Levites, Num. 4:11-13, 40-51).

"By faith Abraham, being tried, offered up Isaac: yea, he that had gladly received the promises was offering up his only begotten *son; even he* to whom it was said, In Isaac shall thy seed be called: accounting that God *is* able to raise up, even from the dead; from whence he did also in a figure receive him back" (Heb. 11:17-19).

CHAPTER FOUR

BIBLICAL THEOLOGY AND THE CONTENT OF PREACHING

BIBLICAL THEOLOGY furnishes a charter for preaching, a declaration of the authority, urgency, and relevancy of preaching Christ from the Scriptures. The preacher who finds in this approach a fresh calling to his labors in the gospel will also discover in biblical theology the key to new richness in sermon content.

To urge the importance of biblical theology as a method in sermon preparation may arouse misgivings, heightened perhaps by the very enthusiasm of those who have recently acquired a taste for this viewpoint. Since a homiletician named Carpzovius produced a volume of one hundred sermon plans three centuries ago[1] there has been no lack of sermon methods. But biblical theology is not a method in this sense. If its principle is grasped, it cannot be optional or superficial. Its approach is rather an essential step in the interpretation of the Bible. Neither exegesis on the one hand, nor systematic theology on the other, can ignore the progressive unfolding of revelation in the history of redemption, and it is the task of biblical theology to study that revelation without losing sight of either its continuity or its progressive and epochal structure.

In tracing the progress of revelation, biblical theology rests upon the unity of the primary authorship of Scripture and the organic continuity of God's work in redemption and revelation. The Old Testament saints looked forward to Messiah's day; they saw it and were glad. We, too, who know Christ's finished work which brought in the end of the ages,

---

1. J. B. Carpzovius, *Hodegeticum*, 1656. Cf. T. Hoekstra, *Gereformeerde Homiletiek*, p. 81.

look forward to the blessed hope of his appearing. We await that day when we shall sit down with Abraham, Isaac, and Jacob in the kingdom of God. No racial memory, no cultural tradition, no transmission of religious experience, nothing that is of man and by men could account for the radical continuity of revelation which we find in the Scriptures.

On the other hand, the periodic or epochal structure of this revelation is also determinative of biblical theology. It is this truth which modern dispensationalism has distorted by permitting the diversity to prejudice the unity, as though God had a succession of plans for man's salvation rather than one great plan moving by epochal strides to the consummation. As we approach the interpretation of the text, we must understand the text in the light of the "theological horizon." As we have seen, the objective unfolding of the events must be understood in unity with the subjective response of faith or of unbelief, and this in terms of the stage of redemption and revelation which has been reached.

The method of biblical-theological preaching involves simply the proper use of these principles in the explanation of the sermon text. Its perspective clarifies the meaning of the text, emphasizes its central message, and provides for sound application. It does not of itself furnish sermonic structure ready-made, although its effect on both homiletical content and form is often revolutionary.

In developing the biblical-theological interpretation of a text, the aspects of epochal structure and continuity may be separately considered. The first step is to relate the text to its immediate theological horizon. This is to carry the principle of contextual interpretation to the total setting of the revelation of the period. It is a step which homiletical hermeneutics cannot afford to overlook. The second step is to relate the event of the text, by way of its proper interpretation in its own period, to the whole structure of redemptive history; and in that way to us upon whom the ends of the ages have come. It must be stressed that this second step is valid and fruitful only when it does come second. All manner of arbitrariness and irresponsibility enter in when we seek to make a direct and practical reference to ourselves without considering the passage in its own biblical and theological setting.

As we relate biblical theology to the content of our preaching, let us consider somewhat more fully each of these steps.

The Text in Its Historical Period

In the first place, then, how may we understand the text in the light of the theological horizon in which it is found? When we map out the field of revelation (to use Vos's phrase), we discover that the great epochal periods are quite evident: the period from the creation to the fall, which we may speak of as the Edenic period; the antediluvian period from the fall to the flood; the period from the flood to the call of Abraham, often referred to as the Noachian epoch; the patriarchal age from Abraham to Moses; the period from Moses to Christ when God deals with the theocracy. The coming of Christ brings in the latter days, the last great period of redemptive history. But the consummation is not yet. It will mark the end of this period and the summing up of all things in Christ.

Within this grand periodic structure of revelation there are many sub-periods which must be noted and understood. The bulk of Old Testament revelation falls within the Mosaic period, which is itself divided into two major eras, the institution of the kingship marking the dividing point. These eras may be still more particularized. In the time of the theocratic kingdom, for example, the separation of the ten northern tribes from Judah after the death of Solomon was much more than a disastrous incident in the politics of Palestine. This breach in the kingdom is of biblical-theological significance, to be noted especially in connection with the ministry of the prophets to Israel in the north. Even greater theological significance attaches to the events of the exile and the restoration. Since each incident is set in an ever-expanding series of horizons that reach to the great epochs of biblical revelation, it is well for the preacher to develop first the more immediate horizon found in the setting of the text, and then to relate this to the broad epochal structure of Scripture.

Such an event as the healing of Naaman by Elisha (I Kings 5) must be seen in relation to the broad horizon of the theocratic kingdom. It must also be seen in relation to the specific setting of the ministry of Elisha. Elisha's ministry is distinct from Elijah's but forms a unity with it. The mantle of Elijah is upon Elisha. We must understand the biblical-theological perspective given in the Lord's commission to Elijah at Horeb: "And Jehovah said unto him, Go, return on thy way, to the wilderness of Damascus: and when thou comest, thou shalt anoint Hazael to be king over Syria; and Jehu the son of Nimshi shalt thou anoint to be king over Israel; and Elisha the son of Shaphat of Abelmeholah shalt thou anoint to be prophet in thy room. And it shall come to pass, that him that escapeth from the sword of Hazael shall Jehu slay; and him that escapeth from the sword of Jehu shall Elisha slay. Yet will I leave *me* seven thousand in Israel, all the knees which have not bowed unto Baal, and every mouth which hath not kissed him" (I Kings 19:15-18).

In the perspective of this commission it is apparent that the ministry of Elijah, continued by Elisha, is one of judgment. Here as in the later prophets, the Word summons the nations to be instruments of God's wrath in judging Israel. This theme goes back to the curses of Ebal and culminates in the prophetic predictions of exile. Such judgments involve a measure of blessing toward the nations, in part as a rebuke to Israel. But since the nations do not serve as instruments of wrath in submission to God, but in proud unbelief, judgment must extend to them as well (Isa. 10:5-19; Jer. 25:29; Obad. 15, 16). Judgment is therefore ultimate and universal.

Yet judgment implies the deliverance of the faithful remnant. The scourges raised up against apostate Israel bring relief to those who have not bowed the knee to Baal. God's purposes do not end in the obliteration of his promises in the fire of wrath. After disobedience has exchanged the blessing for a curse, God will restore his people from captivity and circumcise their hearts (Deut. 30:1, 6; Jer. 31:31-34). The blessing of the people of God in the latter days will be manifested to the nations and shared by them in the fulfillment of the promises to Abraham (e.g. Isa. 2:2-4; 56:6-8; Zech. 14:16-19; Ps. 47:9). In Isaiah this prophetic picture reaches its climax in the description of the salvation of Israel wrought by the Suffering Servant, in whom Israel comes to the fullfillment of its universal calling (Isa. 49:5, 6).

This ultimate messianic reference does not have the same focus in the ministry of Elijah and Elisha which it gained in the later prophets. It is by no means absent, however. These solitary men of God fill a heightened role in contrast with false prophets, spurious priests, and apostate kings, a role which strikingly anticipates the position of the Messiah as the Father and defense of Israel (cf. II Kings 2:12; 13:14). The miraculous ministry exercised by them is a sign of this ultimate vindication of the word of God.

The function of Elijah and Elisha introduces, then, the great prophetic theme of judgment on Israel through the nations, with blessing to the Gentiles as one of its consequences.

The ministry of Elijah to the widow of Zarephath (I Kings 17) is an indication of this kind, as our Lord reminded the Jews of Nazareth (Luke 4:25, 26). The ministry of Elisha to Naaman also fits into this pattern. It is the sign of a prophet in Israel. Judgment toward apostate Israel is indicated in this great mercy made known toward the captain of the enemy host. The sign of mercy toward the Gentiles is extended. The mighty Naaman, an unclean Gentile, a defiled leper, is brought from the heathen court of Ben-hadad to the people of God. That witness to the nations which should have been given by unfaithful Israel, the servant of the Lord, will be given by the prophet who is a true servant of the Lord. So Naaman is brought from the court of Jehoram, representing an apostate theocracy, to the house of Elisha, the prophet of God. Yet he is not cleansed by the hand of the prophet, or in the house of the prophet. His cleansing comes by the word of God.

The sign of God's sovereign salvation thus wrought upon this Gentile has an obverse side in the narrative, for the sign of God's sovereign judgment, also wrought by his word, comes upon Gehazi. The balance of this narrative does not simply indicate that salvation cannot be bought, as Naaman hoped, nor sold, as Gehazi supposed. Nor does it merely show the goodness and the severity of God. In the biblical-theological setting, the relation of Israel to the Gentiles cannot be ignored. The anointing of Hazael and the restoration of Naaman are part of the consistent picture of judgment upon Israel and blessing to the Gentiles.

Our hermeneutical method, therefore, must always begin by finding the immediate theological horizon and then relating that to the broader biblical-theological perspectives. When this is done, the specific force of the text in its horizon will become evident. Each event of redemption, each portion of God's revelation, makes its distinctive contribution to the whole. When we choose a text from Scripture, we do not arbitrarily impose a unity upon the Word of God. We discover the unity that is already present. That unity is already articulated into larger and larger unities in the organic interrelationships of Scripture.

As an example, let us note how the prophecy of Jonah relates to the horizons of biblical theology and how it makes its own specific contribution. It would be altogether superficial to judge that Jonah's prophecy is a strange exception to a uniform particularism of the Old Testament. Even in the Abrahamic period of revelation there comes, along with the development of particularism of grace, a revelation that in Abraham's seed all the nations of the earth will be blessed. The setting up of the seed of Abraham is a particularistic means to a universal end of blessing. Even in this period it is to be noted that this blessing has an eschatological position. It is connected with the seed (Gen. 17:7), which, as Paul reminds us, is not the many, but the one, that coming One whose day Abraham saw and was glad (Gal. 3:16).

It is the Mosaic period, however, which forms the background for Jonah's prophecy. In this period, through sovereign, electing grace, and by the outstretched arm of God's redemption, the theocracy was brought into being. It was established on the basic covenantal principle that this people was God's own possession (Exod. 19:5). The nation was a religious and not an ethnic entity. God's covenant presence established them as a people (Exod. 33:16). The theocratic law upon which the institutions of Israel were founded was a revelation from God. The people were to obey it in the very presence of God, as the mighty words "before me" in Exodus 20:2 remind us. The theocratic institutions all derive from the presence of God in the midst. It is this principle which determines the cultus and necessitates the mediatorial offices of Moses and Aaron, the Levites, and the judges. The government of the people is the theocratic rule of God who dwells in the midst.

From this covenantal organization of the people there derives its relation to the nations. God is the God of Israel. Israel is both the son of God and the servant of God; it has a theocratic mission to perform. The structure of the book of Genesis, relating as it does the call of Abraham to God's dealings with all mankind, gives the setting of this mission. Israel is God's servant in dealing with all of the nations. In particular, this mission has a direct relation to the eschatology of the Abrahamic promises. "Now therefore, if ye will obey my voice indeed, and keep my covenant, then ye shall be mine own possession from among all peoples: for all the earth is mine: and ye shall be unto me a kingdom of priests, and a holy nation" (Exod. 19:5, 6). This mission of Israel includes the duty of sanctifying God's name before all the peoples (cf. Deut. 28:10).

The theocratic distinctiveness of Israel is related to this theocratic mission. Israel must be *religiously* distinct, maintaining the first table of the law. The true God must be

worshipped exclusively, and God must be worshipped spiritually. In the second table of the law the *ethical* distinctiveness
of Israel is apparent. Israel must obey God as over against
the abominations of the heathen (Lev. 18:24-30). The *ceremonial* distinctiveness of Israel also reflects the covenant
principle. Israel is separated to the Holy God who dwells
among them. God's dwelling with his people is the ground
for the ceremonial separation indicated by the concept of
cleanness. The *geographical* distinctiveness of Israel is also
related to its witness. Israel is called to dwell in a land in
the midst of the nations where God's dwelling is established,
and to which all the peoples should turn in receiving the true
God (Deut. 11:32; cf. 12:5).

The kingdom represents a development within the theocratic
concept. The name of God is established in Jerusalem, the
political capital where the throne of David is. The development of the prosperity of the kingdom manifests the glory of
God's name. This development includes the fulfillment of
the divine command in conquering the surrounding enemies
and possessing territory promised to the patriarchs (I Kings
4:21; cf. Gen. 15:18). Note that indefinite expansion is not
promised. Israel is not to embark on wars of conquest to
achieve world dominion. The ideal is rather of a flourishing
kingdom in God's land in the midst of the nations. The
priestly function of Israel is still prominent. With God's
name set in Jerusalem the land becomes a permanent en-
campment of Israel among the nations of the world.

The fullest realization of this ideal comes in the time of
Solomon. David's victories brought the land to its promised
extent. The building of the temple established God's name in
the midst of his people (cf. Deut. 12:5; I Kings 8:16-21).
With the realization of these promises Solomon eloquently
expresses the universalism of the kingdom ideal in his dedica-
tory prayer for the temple (I Kings 8:41-43, 60). "That all
the peoples of the earth may know thy name to fear thee,
as doth thy people Israel . . ." (v. 44). "That all the peoples

of the earth may know that Jehovah is God, there is none else" (v. 60).

The summit of the realization of the theocratic kingdom ideal under Solomon was no sooner attained, however, than it was lost. The sin of king and of people brought about a division of the kingdom, and the covenant was broken. The breaking of the covenant brought the judgment of God. We have already noted in connection with the ministry of Elisha to Naaman the structure of this judgment. If Israel will not witness to all of the nations of the earth by obedience to the covenant, then that witness will be borne through the divine wrath poured out upon Israel. With this judgment there comes blessing to the nations.

The universalism of Jonah is connected with this theme. Jonah prophesied perhaps as early as 800 B.C. It is noted in II Kings 14:25 that certain prophecies of Jonah respecting the restoration of territory to Israel were fulfilled in the reign of Jeroboam II. These prophecies spoke of relief from grievous oppression, which may have referred to Hazael (cf. II Kings 13:22, 23). The reign of Jereboam II was one of great outward prosperity. The words of Jonah were fulfilled. The attacks of the Assyrians weakened the power of Damascus, then Assyrian power itself entered a period of decline. But the deliverances God granted to Israel were not received by the people as occasions for thanksgiving and for repentance. Rather, Jonah's promises of deliverance had to be followed by Amos' denunciations and predictions of exile.

The reference in II Kings 14:25 helps us to understand the book of Jonah. Since the prophet ministered in the period after the extermination of Baal worship, and was given a message of deliverance for Israel, it is easy to understand the hopes he cherished for his nation. But the enemy to be feared was Assyria. The Assyrians had compelled Jehu to pay heavy tribute, as we learn from the Black Obelisk of Shalmaneser III; Jonah would therefore regard Assyria and its captial city of Nineveh as a dangerous threat to the future security of Israel.

The book of Jonah resembles the books of the former prophets. It records history, but not of the covenant nation or of the life of the prophet. Rather it records one commission given by God to Jonah and how it was discharged.

The startling aspect of the commission is its directive to a Gentile city. From the time of Abraham God's revelation had been directed to the covenant people. The office of the prophet was a theocratic institution. The prophet was like unto Moses, bringing the Word of God to the people of God. The great significance of the book of Jonah is grasped only against the background of God's relations to a covenant-breaking people. Through sin the nation had been divided; from its very inception the northern kingdom was guilty of idolatry. The ministry of Elijah and Elisha, God's great appeal to the northern kingdom, was heeded by only a remnant. Although Baalism was checked by Elijah and exterminated outwardly by Jehu, idolatry, immorality, and apostasy abounded. Soon the judgments of the law of Moses must descend. Jonah's own prophecies of political expansion pointed to a last opportunity for the people to manifest a repentance in prosperity which they had not shown in affliction. The exile was only a generation away.

The book of Jonah stands in the midst of the prophetic presentation of blessings to the Gentiles in connection with judgment upon Israel. In the ministry of Elijah and Elisha, the widow of Zarephath and Naaman were brought as Gentiles to taste of the prophetic blessings. On the other hand, Elisha was also commissioned to anoint Hazael king of Damascus, and Elisha journeyed to Damascus to bring the word of God to him. The prophet of Israel was thus used of God to raise up a scourge, not only against the house of Ahab, but also against the nation of Israel.

The commission to Jonah stands in significant relation to the anointing of Hazael. The scourge of Damascus had been removed. Jonah had prophesied and perhaps already seen the resulting political expansion. But a new adversary was to be raised up. As Elisha was sent to Damascus, Jonah was sent to

Nineveh. It was with bitter grief that Elisha brought the word of God to Hazael (II Kings 8:11-13). So also, Jonah viewed with dismay the sparing of Nineveh, particularly when it was to have been destroyed in forty days!

Jonah's commission thus forms a connecting link between God's word to Elijah on Horeb regarding the raising up of Hazael, and the prediction of the invading Assyrians in Amos and Hosea. God judges his people by raising up the heathen against them.

But the other aspect of the message of the prophet is not only present but prominent in Jonah. The mercies of God are extended to the Gentiles. Here also there is implied a strong rebuke to Israel, the Israel of that day and of a later day. "The men of Nineveh shall stand up in the judgment with this generation, and shall condemn it: for they repented at the preaching of Jonah; and behold, a greater than Jonah is here" (Matt. 12:41).

Jonah's mission to Nineveh was not simply to preserve an avenging enemy for Israel; neither was it merely to dramatize and rebuke the unbelief of the people by means of the contrast between the ready response of Nineveh to a single prophetic proclamation on the one hand, and Israel's stubborn rejection of the repeated and continued ministrations of the prophets on the other. The manifestation of God's mercy toward Nineveh is of primary importance in Jonah's mission. This is a manifestation in history of that other theme which the prophets emphasized in connection with the exile. The blessing of Abraham will be carried to the nations. To be sure, Jonah's work at Nineveh was not the declaration of the whole counsel of God to the heathen. It was rather one brief, limited call to repentance. But it did manifest the power of God's word among the heathen, and, more particularly, the mercy of God toward them.

The personal history of the prophet Jonah both illustrates and symbolizes these truths. The mercy of God shown toward his prophet prepares us to understand his mercy extended to the men of Nineveh. The primary truth of redemption recognized at the close of Jonah's psalm (salvation is of the Lord — Jonah 2:9) is evident in God's purposes of mercy shown through the whole book and specifically applied to the men of Nineveh at its conclusion (4:11).

The deliverance of Jonah from the deep manifests the power of God to save from death and symbolizes the resurrection. Such a message has comfort not only for the individual servant of God: it applies also to his people as a whole. Here also the book Jonah prepared for the exile. Buried in the sea of the nations, Israel was not cut off completely. Because salvation is of the Lord, his people would emerge from their captivity to carry forward his work and proclaim his word to the nations.

Thus the typical foreshadowing of the resurrection of Christ (Matt. 12:38-40; 16:4; Luke 11:29-32) is not an isolated aspect of the history of Jonah. Jonah as the individual servant of the Lord represents the whole nation called to be God's servant. His judgment, deliverance, and mission are pregnant with meaning against the background of the calling of the people of God. This connection is not arbitrary but inescapable, particularly in relation to the corporate solidarity evident in the Old Testament. In this way Jonah is a type of Christ, the Head of the people and the Suffering Servant, who bore the judgment, emerged victorious in the resurrection, and discharged the mission in which the people failed.

The Text in God's Total Revelation

In the remarks just made we have come to a consideration of the second major step in the use of the biblical-theological method for interpreting texts of Scripture. Once the text is seen in terms of its own theological horizon, and the more immediate theological context is related to the broader structure of the period of that revelation, we are ready to proceed to a consideration of the relation of the text to the whole of revelation and its significance for us. This means that the Old Testament theology must be related to the New, and that within New Testament theology we must become aware of the divisions that are made by the work of our Lord: his incarnation, crucifixion, resurrection, and ascension.

The relation of the New Testament to the Old is eschatological; all the promises are fulfilled in the "last days" by the coming of the Lord. In his presence the covenant is realized and sealed. Fundamentally, therefore, there are but two epochs, the "former days" and the "latter days," the era before Christ and that which is dated "anno Domini." Since the latter includes the interim between the first and second coming of Christ it embraces fulfillment which is not yet openly manifest, although it is realized in Christ. We do not yet see all things subject to him, "But we behold him who hath been made a little lower than the angels, even *Jesus*, because of the suffering of death crowned with glory and honor . . . ." (Heb. 2:9).

In interpreting the revelation of the "former days" as it focuses on Christ we must bear in mind the principles we have already considered. Christ is revealed in the Old Testament both as Lord and as Servant. His revelation as the Lord is direct; the grace which is shown in his coming and dwelling with his people in theophanic glory is the same grace which is fully manifest in the incarnation. The exercise of that saving lordship results in the realization of the covenant promise, which is nothing short of life in God's presence forever. Old Testament saints were made citizens of the heavenly Zion by faith, and New Testament believers are added to the same great heavenly assembly of saints and angels (Eph. 2:12, 19; Heb. 11:14-16; 12:22-23; Matt. 8:11, 12).

However, just because the final redemption is accomplished in history by the incarnate Son of God, the saving work of the Lord in the Old Testament is not complete. It has a prospective reference pointing forward to the great day of culmination. The Old Testament people of God are saved in hope, rejoicing in the promises seen afar off, and acknowledging that they without us could not be made perfect (Heb. 11:13, 40; cf. I Pet. 1:12).

This provisional aspect of the Old Testament revelation of the lordship of Christ is even more evident in the revelation of his work as Servant. When Israel is saved and judged through the Old Testament men of God, this work can only anticipate the true salvation to be wrought by Christ. It is indeed the Spirit of the Lord who comes upon these men of God, yet the central work of redemption is not theirs to accomplish. Even Moses is but a servant in the house of God, preparing for the coming of the Son (Heb. 3:1-6).

Because of the continuity of God's work of redemption, the connection between salvation in the Old Testament and the New is organic. There is one saving Lord, and one true Israel, the people of God. But because of the epochal progression of redemption and revelation to fulfillment in Christ, there is a dependence of the partial on the total, of the provisional on the final, of the old on the new. In the form of revelation, therefore, the principle of analogy operates. The essence of the covenant is the same, and only in Christ is it actualized: I will be your God, and ye shall be my people. By faith, by a "realized eschatology," believers in all ages share this covenant relation, and their experience of fellowship with God is actual; their life is not a parable of salvation but the experience of it. Yet the redemptive manifestation of God to which faith is directed culminates in Christ, and redemption and revelation in the earlier ages foreshadow Christ.

Symbolism

In this structure of redemptive history symbolism operates with a double reference. Until the heavenly reality is manifested, the covenant fellowship is mediated through earthly symbols, "like in pattern" to the heavenly archetype (Heb. 9:24, 25). With the coming of grace and truth in Christ the reality to which the symbol pointed is revealed. It is not only in retrospect that the reference to Christ is established. Because of the promise aspect of the covenant, the faith that rested in the heavenly realization of earthly symbols

55230

also looked forward to the manifestation in history of the same divine reality (cf. Heb. 11:10, 13-16, 26).

It is important to note that the eschatological realization of redemption is not a symbol, but the actuality. This is the meaning of the emphasis in John's Gospel on the realization of truth (*aletheia*) in Jesus Christ (e.g. John 1:17). The incarnation is not a symbolic dwelling of God with men. Rather, the glory of God which appeared in the symbolic cloud above the symbolic tent is now really present (John 1:14).

It is evident, then, that symbolism is of particular importance in relating the revelation of the "past ages" to the fulfillment in Christ. Symbols abound in Scripture, not incidentally, but because of the structure of the history of redemption which is at once organic and progressive.

Any brief treatment of symbolism is in immediate danger of foundering in the tempest of modern controversy: in philosophy, aesthetics, cultural anthropology, linguistic studies, and not least in modern theology the issue of symbolism is central. The preacher can scarcely be competent in all these areas, but he must have working principles for the interpretation of biblical symbolism.

Contemporary discussion certainly should warn us against underestimating the importance of symbols. Any naive repugnance to the "oriental imagery" of the Bible fails to take account of the symbolism in all speech and life. The most literally-minded scientist becomes surprisingly oriental in his dreams![2] Indeed, science itself is a triumph of symbolism; the equations of modern physics have replaced the models of Newtonian days, but the symbolical function has become so much the more evident. Ernst Cassirer has said that "instead of defining man as an *animal rationale*, we should define him as an *animal symbolicum*."[3] Symbols as

2. Cf. Cyril Richardson, "The Foundations of Christian Symbolism," in F. Ernest Johnson, ed., *Religious Symbolism* (N. Y.: Harper, 1955), p. 2.

3. *Essay on Man* (New Haven: Yale University Press, 1944), p. 26.

distinct from signals are the mark of human thought, in Cassirer's view.

Students of linguistics who have analyzed the symbolic function of language have called attention to the "faded metaphors" that fill our speech and furnish the material of its development.[4] The preacher who would plough under all the symbolism of Scripture in favor of a bare "literalism" should be prepared to assert not only that God has eyes, but that these eyes have legs, since they "run to and fro through all the earth" (Zech. 4:10).

Of course, the most extreme literalist would indignantly declare that his rule is to be "literal where possible" and that we are compelled to take anthropomorphic descriptions of God figuratively. The canon "literal where possible" is itself a confession of bias, although an ineffective one, for it does not even serve to defend against the reduction of all of revelation to myth. Bultmann could claim to be "literal where possible"; he simply cannot regard the supernatural as possible, so he would salvage an existential message by way of symbolism.

The interpreter, and certainly the preacher, should carry no such prejudice against symbolism. The concreteness and imaginative appeal of symbolism is the glory of language. The richness of scriptural symbols which pervades our hymns should give power to the pulpit as well.

The fear of symbolism and the desire for literalism cannot be set aside, however, by a simple appeal to the universality of symbolic forms. It is the question of meaning which is at issue. It may be granted that every word is a symbol and that language itself is therefore totally symbolic in form. It is another question, however, whether the meaning of language must be limited by its form. It is not surprising that semantical theory has often insisted that the term "God" is meaningless. The semanticist is only reading back the presuppositions of his own approach, which restricts meaning

4. Cf. Susanne K. Langer, *Philosophy in a New Key* (Cambridge, Mass.: Harvard University Press, 1957), pp. 140f.

to the experimentally verifiable. In appreciating the structure of symbolism the Christian does not accept the skeptical doctrine that human experience is ultimate. It is part of the wonder of the creation of man in God's image that the creature who knows by analogy in the discursive process of temporal thought nevertheless is able to know the revealed truth of God. It is this which delivers theology from mere shadow-play with symbols of human thought that are held to be empty of the absolute truth they purport to declare.

The desire for literal interpretation of Scripture reflects a proper conviction as to the revealed truth of the Word of God. Its suspicion of symbolism, however, overlooks the precision of meaning which symbolism may convey. In view of the history of biblical interpretation this oversight is understandable. Symbolism has been notoriously abused by the most fanciful misinterpretation. Free rein was given to arbitrary allegorization because no clear principles for interpreting the meaning of symbolism were maintained.

Yet symbolism does have meaning, and it is the duty of the interpreter to grasp it. The most precise "literal" meaning is conveyed by the symbolism of language itself. To be sure, a word is a symbol with a firm denotation and a structured connotation; its reference is more evident than is the symbolism of a fresh metaphor. Yet a metaphor also has definite meaning, with a denotation fixed by the subject and the context. Figurative language makes meaningful statements. When Jesus said "I am the door" he stated something quite definite about his unique mediatorial role. To understand his meaning it is necessary to discover the precise point of the comparison, to grasp the function of the door in the sheepfold and the respect in which Jesus' work is analogous to this function. This may be interpreted rightly or wrongly, but the statement cannot be dismissed as "merely figurative."

Interpreting Biblical Symbols

It may be helpful, then, to note some evident principles for the interpretation of biblical symbols. *First*, we should recognize that the symbol is distinct from that which it represents. The Roman Catholic view of transubstantiation passes beyond symbolism at the point of the elevation of the host. If the bread becomes the body of Christ it can no longer represent it. In biblical theology, as we have seen, the realization of the promises in Christ is not in symbol, but reality. In the Old Testament, on the other hand, a symbolic aspect, anticipating the climactic work of Christ, attaches to every manifestation of the saving power of God. The exodus deliverance of the people of God is a great figure of salvation. For some who passed through the sea it may have been the decisive seal of faith; they may have experienced the inward reality of the salvation of the covenant even as they enjoyed this outward realization. Yet many who were thus delivered through the sea perished in the wilderness in unbelief. The exodus deliverance was not in itself the salvation which it symbolized.

Similarly, the outward judgments of God in the history of redemption are not yet the final judgment. Moses, too, must die in the wilderness in divine judgment, but his name is not blotted from the book of life.

Even in the New Testament the distinction between symbol and reality continues. Although the reality is present in Christ, there are stages in his redemptive work. His miracles are still signs of the kingdom. The resurrection life given to Lazarus is not yet the life of glory; Lazarus is still subject to death. The miracles are signs of the new creation, but they are not yet the re-creation of him who is the resurrection and the life.

To be sure, the reality which is symbolized is often present to faith; the blessing of Christ which brings healing often pronounces eternal peace upon the healed. Yet clear understanding of symbolism always requires that the distinction between the symbol and its referent be maintained.[5]

Second, there must be a relation between the symbol and

5. Cf. Meredith G. Kline, "The Intrusion and the Decalogue," *Westminster Theological Journal,* XVI (1953), 1-22.

the reality symbolized. Undergirding the structure of relation is the creative and providential power of God. R. B.
Kuiper has pointedly remarked that the position of the
adjectives in the title of Henry Drummond's *Natural Law in
the Spiritual World* should be reversed. God is the Father
from whom every created "fatherdom" is named (Eph.
3:14, 15). The rich fruitfulness of symbolism flows from the
relatedness of our thought and experience as it responds to
the creative Word of God. The organic unity-in-diversity
of the human body is a powerful symbol of the church because
both are the work of God; it is the Creator Spirit whose work
reveals the order of divine wisdom united to the power of
the living God. The union of husband and wife symbolizes
the relation of Christ and his church in a fashion that is still
more meaningful, for here the richest expression of human
fellowship points to union with him whose Image is its ground.
This divinely appointed structure of relation is not identity,
however. The symbol remains a symbol, and frightful idolatry arises when the highest symbols are identified with that
which they symbolize. It is significant that washing and
eating rather than sexual intercourse are the functions in
which the sacraments are appointed. The limitation of the
symbol is thus the more evident, although even those sacraments have been made idolatrous.

The relation which gives meaning to symbolism is not
limited to these rich and complex modes of human experience
connected with physical and social life. All the categories of
thought and experience offer relations which symbolism may
use. An object may become a symbol through a play on
words, the connection consisting merely in a similarity of
sound between the name of the object and the concept
which it symbolizes.[6]

Third, the reference of the symbols of Scripture is divinely
established in revelation. Susanne K. Langer has distinguished

---

6. So, for example, in Jeremiah 1:11, where the vision of the rod of an
almond tree (Heb. *shaqedh*) symbolizes the word of Jehovah "I
watched [Heb. *shoquedh*] over my word to perform it."

between the discursive symbolism of mathematics and language and "presentational" symbolism. In the latter category she would place not only the symbolism of art and music, but also that of the rites and myths of religion.[7] Presentational symbolism has meaning, she holds, but it is not meaning which can be reduced to discursive language or thought. There are many who regard biblical religion as a poetic mythology, expressing through intuitive and imaginative forms the reality of man's encounter with the Absolute. They would be hesitant to "demythologize" lest there be found nothing for thought to grasp of this encounter.

The biblical theology of revelation, however, cannot be set at a convenient distance from science in this way. The symbolism of Scripture is communicated in word revelation, and its elements have rational meaning. Indeed, the symbolism of Scripture is characteristically discursive rather than presentational. Rather than there being a wholeness of imagery which baffles thought, the symbolism is organized coherently and conceptually. Not the imaginative details nor the *Gestalt* of vision are brought to the fore, but the conceptual significance. The contrast between the conduct of Elijah and the priests of Baal on Carmel epitomizes the distinctiveness of biblical religion in this respect, though even Baalism now appears to have been more conceptual than the advocates of "primitive mentality" ever imagined!

It is not the poetic ambiguity of scriptural symbols which gives them power; nor is it the exemplification of the archetypal imagery of the unconscious. Rather, it is the truths which they express. Deliberate ambiguity as a literary form is sometimes found. Vos has pointed out the literary effectiveness of Isaiah's term for the idols (*elilim*) which means things of nought, but also suggests Elohim, and the diminutive of El, that is, "godlets."[8] Cullmann has shown the double meaning of such terms as "above/anew" and "lifted up" in

7. *Op. cit.*, ch. 4, "Discursive and Presentational Forms."
8. Vos, *Biblical Theology*, p. 255.

John.[9] Scriptural symbols do grip the imagination, as centuries of Christian poetry attest. But the symbol is never primary or ultimate. The symbols do not fill the horizon of experience but gain their meaning from the context. Very often many separate and varied symbols are used in one context to convey one pattern of ideas. It has often been pointed out, for example, that the symbolic language in which Christ is described in Revelation 1 is not such as to present one imaginative whole. Rather, it is a mosaic of concrete symbolic meanings, which, interpreted in the light of Old Testament revelation, presents an overpowering picture of Christ in his priestly-kingly glory as he addresses his Word to the churches. The imagery serves the meaning; it is not sovereign in its own dimension.

Even in sacramental symbolism the additional factor does not lie in any mystic dimension of the symbolic act, and far less in an identity of the symbol with the reality, but rather in the fact that the appropriation of salvation is symbolized, and that the symbol is therefore a seal of participation in the promised blessing.[10]

The interpreter of biblical symbols needs therefore to seek the meaning of the individual elements of symbolism in the context of scriptural use. As in all exegesis the historical setting must be examined. The whole context of the period of revelation is always significant. Thus the "ladder" of Jacob's dream is linked by the phrase "the top of it reached to heaven" (Gen. 28:12) with the tower of Babel (Gen 11:4) and symbolizes God's visitation in grace by the means of his appointing; in contrast we have the edifice of men's vain worship, which could only bring God's visitation of judgment. The ziggurat tower from the cultural setting of the patriarchal period underlies Jacob's dream.

Fourth, the symbols of Scripture may be classified in various groups. Some are provided by God directly: in the

9. Oscar Cullmann, *Early Christian Worship* (Chicago: Regnery, 1953), pp. 50ff.

10. Cf. M. G. Kline, *op. cit.,* p. 5.

manifestation of his covenant presence (the fire in the bush and on Sinai, the stairway at Bethel); in the confirmation of his covenants (the rainbow for the covenant with Noah); in the communication of his message (the visions of Zechariah or Daniel). Usually these divine symbols are emphatically supernatural. Their immediate divine origin makes them "signs" of God's presence and power.

In addition to these there is the large class of what might be called institutional symbols. These are initially cultic in character: God requires of men worship by sacrifice. We find this beginning with Abel, and it is continued through the patriarchal age.

In the establishment of the covenant with Abraham, circumcision is commanded as a symbol which is not simply cultic but institutional, marking out as it does the people of God. With the establishment of the theocratic form of the covenant, not only is the cultus vastly elaborated to express the principle of God dwelling in the midst, but we have also in the priestly, prophetic, and kingly offices institutions which relate to the direction of the whole life of the theocratic nation and which have a symbolic aspect.

A third class of symbols might be called the prophetic. Perhaps this might be regarded as an extension of the first. It includes symbolic actions on the part of the prophets at the command of God, for example, Ezekiel's representation of the seige of Jerusalem or Hosea's marriage to Gomer. The symbolic naming of Isaiah's children is a slightly different instance of this. Symbols which find expression in the language of the Old Testament would also be in this group.

Historical symbols form still a fourth class. These are also closely related to the first. God has not only wrought signs directly and commanded men to observe symbolic rituals, he has also directed the course of the history of salvation in such a way that spiritual realities are symbolized in historical events. As we have seen, this is implicit in the very structure of redemption. In the exodus the various types of symbolism are concentrated about the great redemptive action of the Old Testament. The plagues are direct divine judgments with symbolic aspects. The passover is ritual symbolism; the casting down of Moses' rod, prophetic. In the crossing of the Red Sea we have historical symbolism. God's deliverance symbolized a spiritual redemption in which Israel as God's son was set free to serve him.

In the New Testament there are instances of such historical symbolism in the ministry of our Lord. A clear example is the miraculous catch of fish in connection with the calling of Peter, Andrew, James, and John (Luke 5:1-11). To be sure, this is a miracle and a sign of the presence of the Messiah and the kingdom of God. But it is a miracle in which the action of the disciples is involved. Through the miracle the whole incident gains the force of a parable of the kingdom.

When Jesus came to the shore of the lake that morning the fishermen were indeed a picture of fruitless toil. With nothing to show for their night of labor but torn and dirty nets, they were engaged in the exasperating chore of cleaning and mending them. As we learn from Luke's Gospel, Jesus did not simply call them under such circumstances. Rather, after teaching from Peter's boat, Jesus commanded him to put out into the lake and let down the nets. Peter, the experienced fisherman, after voicing a half protest, obeyed the Teacher and soon both boats were filled to sinking.

It is against this background that Jesus says to these awe-struck men, "Fear not, from henceforth thou shalt catch men." The symbolism of vast success in obedient service of the sovereign Christ is inescapable. We are the more impressed by the repetition of this miracle after the resurrection as the sign by which Jesus made himself known (John 21:1-14).

Instructed by the method of this miracle our eyes are opened to the symbolism of other miracles and events in the life of Christ, who in everything perfectly fulfilled the work the Father gave him to do. When we reflect, for example, on the significance of Jesus' walking on the water we find there is rich symbolism involved. So Jesus always comes in the storm to strengthen the faith of his own.

Particularly in the Gospel of John our attention is drawn to the symbolic character of the miracles of Christ. Oscar Cullmann has given us a convincing demonstration of this, even if we may feel that he sometimes overstates the case for the sacramental reference of the symbolism.[11]

Symbols and Types

This brief consideration of symbolism in Scripture will aid us in a right approach to typology. A simple schematism that is helpful here is to regard symbolism as involving a vertical reference to revealed truth as it is manifested in a particular horizon of redemptive history. Typology is then the prospective reference to the same truth as it is manifested in the period of eschatological realization.

It might be diagrammed as follows:

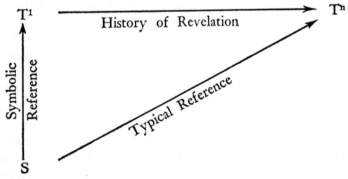

S is the symbol. T^1 is the truth to which it refers, as that truth is manifest in the particular period in question.

The line of the History of Revelation connects this earlier revelation with T^n, the fullness of that truth revealed in Christ. The lines S-T^1 and S-T^n are the reference lines of symbolism and typology respectively. This diagram is of only limited usefulness. But it does make clear that only the symbolic can

11. Cullmann, *op. cit.*

be typical. As Vos says, "The gateway to the house of typology is at the farther end of the house of symbolism."[12] The diagram also indicates that an Old Testament event or institution may be typical only of the truth which it symbolizes. The only difference is the prospective reference of typology to that truth in its New Testament realization.

Thus the offering of the passover lamb symbolizes substitutionary atonement and therefore typifies this aspect of the work of Christ.

It will be observed that as there are both institutional-cultic and historical symbols, so there is corresponding typology. The tabernacle-temple, the sacrificial system, and the sabbatical calendar with its set feasts are all symbolic elements with most significant typical reference. We have already had occasion to note, for example, how Jesus referred to the Isaianic application of the year of jubilee to the messianic age and claimed that this prophecy was fulfilled in himself.

The exodus, the wanderings, and the possession of the land are symbolic events of the redemptive history and have typical reference to the realization of redemption in Christ. The propriety of historical typology is vigorously defended by Patrick Fairbairn in his old, but by no means outmoded, classic on the subject of typology.[13]

Clearer understanding of biblical theology and sharper discernment of the theological horizons of the periods of revelation will aid us in appreciating the symbolism of Scripture. The reverse is also true. If we proceed to construct the line of typology only when we have first clarified the symbolism we will be able to work in confidence. We honor the Word of God when we recognize the principle of organic connection between promise and fulfillment. Such a method does not commend itself to those who deny or de-emphasize the primary authorship of Scriptures. Only the lack of hermeneutical method can shut us up to recognizing types only where

12. Vos, *op. cit.*, p. 162.
13. Patrick Fairbairn, *The Typology of Scripture* (Edinburgh, 1864), 2 vols. Reprint, Grand Rapids: Zondervan, 1952.

the New Testament itself explicitly recognizes them. Such caution is then admirable. But a better grasp of biblical theology will open for us great riches of revelation. We need not lack the sound method to find these and bring them to the people of God.

Perhaps the strongest objection to the use of the biblical-theological approach in preaching is its difficulty. It has been said that this is a scholar's approach to sermons, far beyond the range of the practicing preacher. Once the necessity and fruitfulness of the method is recognized, how-ever, no worthy workman in the Word can refuse the effort it requires. He is called as a scribe of the kingdom to bring forth treasures new and old, and any labor that issues in a fuller preaching of Christ has its reward.

It cannot be denied that scholarship is a necessary ingre-dient in biblical-theological preaching, but this is no less true of any preaching which is more than trite moralizing or emotionalism.

Tools and Methods

A few remarks about tools and methods may be an en-couragement to some to whom this approach might appear forbidding. The layman as well as the preacher can study biblical theology; its basic techniques can be followed to a considerable extent without training in the original languages of Scripture. There is no novelty in the methods that serve biblical theology, although some steps in exegesis assume particular importance.

First, diligent Bible reading is essential. No scholarly tech-nique can be substituted for knowledge of the Bible. The New Testament writers commonly assume in their readers a knowledge of the Old Testament beyond that possessed by many of today's ministers. The points of connection that illuminate the structure of biblical theology may be brought to light by the exhaustive research of the scholar, but they are often evident on the surface to the Christian who knows his Bible. For example, Jesus responds to the claim of the Jews to be Abraham's seed, who have never known bondage, by declaring, "The bondservant abideth not in the house for ever: the son abideth for ever" (John 8:35). It was doubtless evident to the Jews that Jesus was alluding to the contrast between Ishmael and Isaac (Gen. 21:10). Later in the same context Jesus says "Your father Abraham rejoiced to see my day; and he saw it, and was glad" (v. 56). Again, knowledge of the Genesis narrative immediately suggests the emphasis on the laughter of Abraham and Sarah in connection with the birth of Isaac (Gen. 17:17-19; 18:12-15; 21:1-7).

Knowledge of Bible history is particularly important. To the familiarity that comes from the study of the biblical narratives there should be added as much reading as possible in the field of archaeology and Bible backgrounds. This is especially important for the understanding of symbolism. The illumination which archaeology has given to the covenant concept illustrates the fruitfulness of this study for biblical theology.[14]

Careful exegesis has always stressed the usage of biblical language. For biblical theology this is essential. Kittel's *Theological Lexicon*[15] always traces the usage of a term through the Scriptures. Studies of this kind are beginning

14. A bibliography of archaeological works may be found in I. M. Price, O. R. Sellers, and E. L. Carlson, *The Monuments and the Old Testament* (Philadelphia: The Judson Press, 1958) which is itself a valuable survey. The two works edited by James B. Pritchard and published by Princeton University Press, *Ancient Near Eastern Texts* (1950), and *The Ancient Near East in Pictures* (1954), bring first-hand knowledge to the English reader. Conservative surveys in this field include Joseph P. Free, *Archaeology and Bible History* (Wheaton: Van Kampen, 1950); Merrill F. Unger, *Archeology and the Old Testament* (Grand Rapids: Zondervan, 1954); J. A. Thompson, *Archaeology and the Old Testament* (Grand Rapids: Eerdmans, 1957), *Archaeology and the New Testament* (Grand Rapids: Eerdmans, 1960).

15. Gerhard Kittel, ed., *Theologisches Wörterbuch zum Neuen Testament* (Stuttgart: Kohlhammer, 1933-).

to multiply in English.[16] This is an area in which patient individual study is always fruitful. It is a wise method to investigate the usage of the Old Testament terms which lie behind the New Testament vocabulary. Here the Septuagint version of the Old Testament is a supremely important link between the language of the Old Testament and the New.[17] Concordance study is the backbone of this approach. Even a layman has access to profitable study of the use of terms in the original language through the splendid organization of Young's *Concordance*.[18]

One must beware, however, of too rapid scanning of concordance columns. If biblical theology is to be appreciated, reflection must center on the use of a term in a particular period of redemptive history. Certain passages often emerge as definitive for an epoch. For example, the great assembly at Sinai, when the earthly "holy ones" and the heavenly holy hosts are gathered in the presence of God, is definitive for the whole biblical concept of the church as the assembly of

16. Selections from Kittel have been translated in J. R. Coates and H. P. Kingdon, eds., *Bible Key Words*, 2 vols. to date (N. Y.: Harper, 1951, 1958). These studies are also published as individual volumes (London: Adam and Charles Black). Other such studies are: J. J. von Allmen, *A Companion to the Bible* (N. Y.: Oxford University Press, 1958). William Barclay, *A New Testament Wordbook* (London: S.C.M. Press, 1955); *More New Testament Words* (N. Y.: Harper, 1958). Alan Richardson, *A Theological Word Book of the Bible* (London: S.C.M. Press, 1950). W. E. Vine, *Expository Dictionary of New Testament Words*, 4 vols. (London: Oliphants, 1939-1941).

17. G. Abbott-Smith, *A Manual Greek Lexicon of the New Testament* (Edinburgh: T. & T. Clark, third edition, 1937) is of the greatest aid in furnishing in each case the Hebrew terms which are translated by a given Greek word in the Septuagint.

18. Robert Young, *Analytic Concordance to the Bible*, Twentieth American Edition (N. Y.: Funk & Wagnalls, n.d.). For the Hebrew Old Testament there is now available Gerhard Lisowsky, *Konkordanz zum hebräischen Alten Testament* (Stuttgart: Privileg. Württ. Bibelanstalt, 1958); and for the Greek New Testament, Alfred Schmoller, *Handkonkordanz zum griechischen Neuen Testament*, ninth edition (Stuttgart: Privileg. Württ Bibelanstalt, 1951). The latter is particularly convenient in the back of a large-type edition of Nestle's Greek Testament.

the saints (Deut. 9:10; 33:2-5; Ps. 68:1, 7, 8, 17, 26, 27; I Cor. 1:1-3; Heb. 12:18-24; cf. *Hymns* III, 21; XI, 11-12 from the Dead Sea Scrolls[19]). Marginal references are at times surprisingly suggestive. The latest Nestle edition of the Greek Testament is most valuable in this respect: the bold-face printing of Old Testament terminology together with the references in the margin make this a superlative study guide.[20]

Comparison and Contrast

From the study of word usage it is usually only a step to the consideration of similar passages. Sometimes striking similarities of word usage or details will link apparently unrelated sections. For example, Matthew Black recently called attention again to the striking connections between the parable of the Good Samaritan (Luke 10:30-37) and the restoration of the Judean captives to Jericho by the men of Samaria as recorded in II Chronicles 28:8-15.[21] So also, the use of the term "compassion" at the climactic point of this parable connects with its application to Christ elsewhere in the gospels (Matt. 9:36; Luke 7:31), and the ministry of compassion carried out by the Samaritan is closely analogous to the work of God toward the foundling Israel (Ezek. 16:5-14), or, more broadly, to the whole divine shepherding of the scattered and wounded flock, neglected by the false shepherds (the priest and Levite pass by). (Cf. Ezek. 34:1-16, 23, 24; Luke 15:3-7; 19:10.)[22] Still further, since this passage is the reply of Jesus to the question of eternal life, it must be studied in connection with the related proposal of this question by the rich young

---

19. Theodor H. Gaster, *The Dead Sea Scriptures in English Translation* (Garden City, N. Y.: Doubleday Anchor Books, 1956), pp. 138, 178.

20. Eberhard Nestle, ed., *Novum Testamentum Graece* (Stuttgart: Privileg. Württ. Bibelanstalt, 1953).

21. Matthew Black, "The Parables as Allegory," *Bulletin of the John Rylands Library*, XLII (1959-1960), 273ff.

22. Birger Gerhardsson, *The Good Samaritan — The Good Shepherd?* (Lund: Gleerup, 1958). Cf. Ronald S. Wallace, *Many Things in Parables* (Edinburgh: Oliver & Boyd, 1955), pp. 105-111; also appendix, "The Parable and the Preacher," pp. 203-218.

ruler in Luke 18:18-30. And since the reply is a parable, it must be compared with the other parables of Jesus.

Such a procedure will avoid the error of a moralistic understanding of this parable which isolates it from the whole teaching and work of Christ. The love that fulfills the law is not the "love" of a calculating moralism which is pretentiously concerned with the identification of one's neighbor. It is the love of divine compassion, fulfilled in him whom the lawyers called a Samaritan (John 8:48) and exercised in his name by the stewards to whom he has committed the ministry of compassion until his return.

The constant approach in the development of biblical-theological perspective is to examine all similarities and correspondences, no matter how remote they may seem at first, to determine where a genuine identity of principle exists. Then there must follow an equally careful process of distinction. Some similarities are not significant; they are not occasioned by any common organic element in revelation. Even where similarities abound, the precise force of a particular text is always defined by its distinctiveness. A miracle of Christ must be considered in connection with all the miracles of Scripture in their relation to the work of redemption. It must also be distinguished, not only from the miraculous plagues of Moses, but from similar miracles — of Elisha, perhaps, or of Jesus himself.

In studying the miracle at Cana one must be sensitive to the symbolism of water, wine, and the wedding feast. Moses' turning of the water to blood must be recalled. The connection of the ministry of John with the water of purification, and Jesus' presence as the bridegroom (John 3:25-30) help us to understand the force of Jesus' statement to his mother that his hour was not yet come (John 2:4; cf. 7:30; 8:20; 12:23; 13:1). The first sign declares the last feast, when the Lord shall provide the best wine (Isa. 25:6-8).[23]

---

23. Cf. Oscar Cullmann, op. cit., pp. 66-71.

Theme and Divisions

Through the procedure of comparison and distinction the central theme which gives unity to the passage must be discerned. This theme should then provide the core of the sermon structure. The development of the theme in the divisions of the sermon may follow one of two general methods. Where the text is familiar and the thematic concept rich, a more synthetic outline may be used. Aspects of the theme derived from the text as a whole form the divisions. The subdivisions then show how each aspect is found in the text and apply it to the hearers. Where the text is lengthy or unfamiliar the outline should be more analytic; that is, the divisions should summarize sections of the text itself as they relate to the theme of the passage. The subdivisions of such an outline are usually more synthetic, that is, they summarize aspects of that particular section of the text in relation to the main theme.

An example of this second, more analytic approach is the following outline of a sermon on John 12:1-8. The divisions here follow the order of the text closely.

Mary's Memorial of Devotion
John 12:1-8

I. The extravagance of Mary's devotion v. 3
    A. In the gift of her substance
    B. In the gift of herself

II. The folly of Mary's devotion vv. 4-6
    A. To humanistic religion v. 5
    B. To sinful covetousness v. 6

III. The perception of Mary's devotion vv. 7, 8
    A. Her devotion perceived the unique work of Christ v. 7
    B. Her devotion perceived the unique person of Christ v. 8

The more synthetic structure is used in the following sermon outline on Genesis 28:10-22. The two major symbols of this passage, the stairway and the house, serve to represent the two major divisions. They were united in the ziggurat figure, for the ziggurat was both a temple and a divine stairway.[24] In the teaching of the passage they are united in the concept of the covenant intervention or advent of the Lord.

God's Coming Confirms the Covenant to the Exiled Seed
Genesis 28:10-22

I. The stairway of God:

   God's sovereign intervention confirms the covenant

   A. The initiative of God's grace in redemption

   B. The efficacy of God's grace in redemption
   (cf. Babel)

   C. The purpose of God's grace in redemption:
   Past, present, and future of grace

II. The house of God:

   God's gracious presence realizes the covenant

   A. The house of blessing, built by God

   1. Its historical reality: the land and the seed

   2. Its ultimate realization: the land and seed as the house

   B. The house of fellowship, indwelt by God

   1. Glorious presence of God

   2. Worshiping response of Jacob

Concl.: Christ fulfilling the stairway and the house

At times a more synthetic element may be carried even into the subdivisions, but the sermon must always present the actual material of the text. The following outline is an example of this:

The Lord Provides the Wine of the Feast
John 2:1-11

I. His sovereign provision

   A. As the Lord of nature

---

24. Cf. André Parrot, *The Tower of Babel* (N. Y.: Philosophical Library, 1955).

B. As the Lord of history
  1. Above the will of his mother
  2. In the will of his Father: my hour

II. His saving provision
  A. As the Lord of grace
    1. Gracious refusal
    2. Gracious fulfillment: in his hour
  B. As the Lord of glory
    1. The eschatological feast
    2. The feasting Saviour

Often where the divisions are more synthetic they are more general than the theme. They apply to the theme the great perspectives of the work of redemption. The outline below as well as that above indicates this.

Hear Ye Him!
(The Commandment of the Revealed Glory of the Son of God)
Luke 9:28-36

I. Hear ye him: the Son as the prophet of glory
  A. In the glory of his heavenly authority
  B. In the glory of his earthly ministry

II. Hear ye him: The Son as the priest of glory
  A. The supreme Mediator
  B. The final sacrifice

III. Hear ye him: the Son as the king of glory
  A. His own glory
  B. His royal work

Again it should be stressed that the development should be in terms of the text. In the outline just above, for example, the sacrifice of Christ is not discussed in general, but as it is alluded to in the text: the conversation with Moses and Elijah concerning his "exodus" which he must accomplish at Jerusalem (Luke 9:31), the significance of Peter's suggestion of the three tabernacles, the teaching of Jesus to his disciples from this point on concerning his coming death.

It should be observed that a well-constructed outline often suggests an alternative plan in the subdivisions. An outline may often be turned "inside out" by making a recurring pattern in the subdivisions the main division, and subordinating the former main division to it. Thus the subdivisions above present the elements of glory and grace, so that it would be possible to deal first with the glory of Christ as prophet, priest, and king, then with the grace of Christ in these same mediatorial roles. Through the use of this procedure a more synthetic outline may often be developed from a more analytic one.

Attention to sermon structure is important to convey with simplicity the richness of biblical theology.

Biblical-theological preaching both demands and brings this richness and simplicity to our sermons. Through such preaching we reflect the "divers manners" in which God spoke to the fathers in the prophets. We enter with sobriety and reverence the world of scriptural symbolism. Our eyes are lifted from the rainbow in the clouds to the rainbow about the throne. Having seen Aaron the high priest of Israel stand by the altar of incense and enter within the veil to sprinkle the mercy-seat with the blood of the atonement, our understanding is enriched to behold with the eye of faith our great High Priest who has entered no earthly tabernacle like in pattern to the true, but into heaven itself to sprinkle the eternal mercy-seat with his own blood. Having stood at the foot of Mount Sinai that burned with fire and having heard in the blackness and darkness and tempest the dread voice before which Moses did exceedingly fear and quake, we come with freshness of spirit "to mount Zion, and unto the city of the living God, the heavenly Jerusalem, and to innumerable hosts of angels, to the general assembly and church of the firstborn who are enrolled in heaven, and to God the Judge of all, and to the spirits of just men made perfect, and to Jesus the mediator of a new covenant, and to the blood of sprinkling that speaketh better than *that* of Abel" (Heb. 12:22-24).

Yes, to Jesus we come, for with richness of figurative language, wealth of ethical insight, and depth of redemptive-historical grasp we are brought by the Scriptures to Jesus. God who spoke in divers manners has spoken in a Son. What focus is brought to our preaching in this approach! When we hear the cry, "Lift up your heads, O ye gates," we see David again dancing before the ark in the ascent to Jerusalem; but we are borne along by the unity of Scripture to see more, to see the King entering in triumph, not only that earthly Zion where the children sang hosanna, but also ascending to the heavenly Jerusalem where the eternal gates lift up their heads to the King of Glory.

Here is freedom in preaching coupled with faithfulness to the Word of God. Here, too, is a message which comes with freshness from that Word which liveth and abideth, and reaches men's hearts with relevancy and power.

It involves patient and faithful study. It is not a superficial technique but a lifetime direction. But the husbandman that laboreth is the first to partake of the fruits!

A SHORT BIBLIOGRAPHY ON THE SUBJECT OF BIBLICAL THEOLOGY

Floyd V. Filson, "The Unity of the Old and New Testaments — a Bibliographical Survey." *Interpretation,* V (1951), 134-152.

Connolly Gamble, Jr., "The Literature of Biblical Theology: a Bibliographical Study," *Interpretation,* VII (1953), 466-480.

Delbert R. Hillers, "An Historical Survey of Old Testament Theology Since 1922," *Concordia Theological Monthly,* XXIX:8, 9 (Aug., Sept., 1958), 571-594; 664-677.

Archibald M. Hunter, *Interpreting the New Testament, 1900-1950* (Philadelphia: The Westminster Press, 1951).

James M. Robinson, *A New Quest of the Historical Jesus* (Naperville, Ill.: A. R. Allenson, 1959).

Krister Stendahl, "A Report on New Testament Studies 1953-1955," *Harvard Divinity School Bulletin,* XXI (1955-1956), 61-80.

H. G. Wood, "The Present Position of New Testament Theology; Retrospect and Prospect," *New Testament Studies,* IV (1958), 169-182.

The following bibliography furnishes a sample of recent efforts to define biblical theology:

Otto J. Baab, "The Study of Old Testament Theology," in *The Theology of the Old Testament* (New York: Abingdon-Cokesbury, 1949), pp. 13-22.

———, "Old Testament Theology: Its Possibility and Methodology," in H. R. Willoughby, ed., *The Study of the Bible Today and Tomorrow* (Chicago: University of Chicago Press, 1947), pp. 401-418.

James Barr, "The Problem of Old Testament Theology and the History of Religion," *Canadian Journal of Theology,* III (1957), 141-149.

Rudolf Bultmann, "Epilogue" in *Theology of the New Testament* (New York: Scribner's, 1955), II, 237-251; bibliography pp. 259f.

James R. Branton, Millar Burrows, James D. Smart, Robert McAfee Brown, "Our Present Situation in Biblical Theology," *Religion in Life,* XXVI (Winter, 1956-1957), 5-39.

Millar Burrows, *An Outline of Biblical Theology* (Philadelphia: Westminster Press, 1946), pp. 4-6.

Henry J. Cadbury, "The Peril of Archaizing Ourselves," *Interpretation,* III (1949), 331-337. See also reply by G. Ernest Wright, "The Problem of Archaizing Ourselves," pp. 450-459.

Robert C. Dentan, *Preface to Old Testament Theology* (New Haven: Yale University Press, 1950).

Gerhard Ebeling, "The Meaning of Biblical Theology," *Journal of Theological Studies*, N.S., VI (1955), 210-225.

A. J. B. Higgins, "The Growth of New Testament Theology," *The Scottish Journal of Theology*, VI (1953), 275-286.

William A. Irwin, "The Reviving Theology of the Old Testament," *Journal of Religion*, XXV (1945), 235-246.

————, "A Still Small Voice . . . Said, What Are You Doing Here?" *Journal of Biblical Literature*, LXXVIII (1959), 1-12.

Martin Kaehler, "Biblical Theology," in *The New Schaff-Herzog Encyclopedia of Religious Knowledge* (Grand Rapids: Baker Book House, reprint 1952), II, 183-186.

Winston L. King, "Some Ambiguities in Biblical Theology," *Religion in Life*, XXVII (1957-1958), 95-104.

Emil G. Kraeling, "Toward a Biblical Theology?" in *The Old Testament Since the Reformation* (London: Lutterworth Press, 1955), pp. 265-284.

James Muilenburg, "Is There a Biblical Theology?" *Union Seminary Quarterly Review*, XII:4, pp. 29-37.

C. R. North, "Old Testament Theology and the History of Hebrew Religion," *Scottish Journal of Theology*, II (1949), 113-126.

Robert A. Pfeiffer, "Facts and Faith in Biblical History," *Journal of Biblical Literature*, LXX (1951), 1-14.

————, "Current Issues in Old Testament Studies," *Harvard Divinity School Bulletin*, XX (1954-1955), 53-65.

Norman W. Porteous, "Old Testament Theology," in H. H. Rowley, ed., *The Old Testament and Modern Study* (London: Oxford University Press, 1951), pp. 311-344.

————, "Towards a Theology of the Old Testament," *Scottish Journal of Theology*, I (1948), 136-149.

James B. Pritchard, "Some Strange Fruit of Old Testament Criticism," *Religion in Life*, XVIII (1948-1949), 34-47.

H. H. Rowley, *The Unity of the Bible* (London: Carey Kingsgate Press, 1953).

Alan Richardson, *An Introduction to the Theology of the New Testament* (London: S.C.M. Press, 1958), pp. 9-15.

James D. Smart, "The Death and Rebirth of Old Testament Theology," *Journal of Religion*, XXIII (1943), 1-11, 125-136.

D. R. Vicary, "Liberalism, Biblical Criticism, and Biblical Theology," *Anglican Theological Review*, XXXII (1950), 114-121.

Geerhardus Vos, "Introduction: The Nature and Method of Biblical Theology," in *Biblical Theology* (Grand Rapids: Eerdmans, 1948), pp. 11-27.

Amos N. Wilder, "New Testament Theology in Transition," in H. R. Willoughby, *op. cit.*, pp. 419-436.

G. Ernest Wright, "Biblical Theology, Old Testament" and Floyd V. Filson, "Biblical Theology, New Testament," in L. A. Loetscher, ed., *Twentieth Century Encyclopedia of Religious Knowledge* (Grand Rapids: Baker Book House, 1955). I, 156-160

G. Ernest Wright, *God Who Acts; Biblical Theology as Recital* (London: S. C. M. Press, 1952).

Edward J. Young, "What is Old Testament Biblical Theology?" *Evangelical Quarterly*, XXXI (1959), 136-142.

————, *The Study of Old Testament Theology Today* (London: James Clarke, 1958).